# Katharine Hepburn

# Katharine Hepburn

## Her Film & Stage Career

CAROLINE LATHAM

PROTEUS BOOKS

LONDON & NEW YORK

PROTEUS BOOKS is an imprint of
The Proteus Publishing Group

United States
PROTEUS PUBLISHING CO., INC
733 Third Avenue
New York NY 10017

distributed by
THE SCRIBNER BOOK COMPANIES INC
597 Fifth Avenue
New York NY 10017

United Kingdom
PROTEUS (PUBLISHING) LIMITED
Bremar House
Sale Place
London W2 1PT

ISBN 086 276 074 7
ISBN 086 276 075 5

First Published in 1982
© 1982 Caroline Latham & Proteus (Publishing) Limited

Editor Kay Rowley
Art Direction B-blunt & Associates

Photo credits:
Kobal Collection: pages 6, 14, 17, 20, 24, 28, 34, 43, 58, 64-7, 71, 73, 81, 87, 93, 97, 98,
101, 104, 108, 112 & 122
The Gate Cinema Shop, Brunswick Square, London WC1: pages 22, 31, 32, 44, 46,
47, 50, 55, 56, 60, 74, 75, 77, 88 & 111
National Film Archive Stills Library: pages 39, 40, 63, 78, 94, 98 & 102
Burt Glinn/Magnum Photos: pages 70 & 84. Cinema International: page 91
Dennis Stock/Magnum Photos: page 69
Steve Schapiro/Sygma: page 68

Typeset by SX Composing Ltd.
Printed by Printer Industria Grafica sa, Barcelona, Spain.
D.L.B. 29272 – 1982.

6

An early publicity picture.

# 1

# An Overnight Success

*You might have predicted that* young Katharine Hepburn was going to get herself noticed.

Hepburn's childhood was happy, busy – and odd. She was born on November 8, 1909, in Hartford, Connecticut. Kate, as her family always called her (and her friends still do) was the second of six children of an unusual couple. Her father, Dr. Thomas Hepburn, was a noted urologist and surgeon on the staff of Hartford Hospital. He was an outspoken man who alienated many of his fellow physicians by his campaign to educate the public about venereal disease. His wife, Katharine Houghton, came from a prominent Boston family and was active in promoting a number of social causes. She was a suffragette who picketed the White House and planned strategy with her friends Emmeline Pankhurst and Emma Goldman. She was also a crusader for birth control and a disciple of Margaret Sanger. She frequently took young Kate along to meetings and demonstrations, to carry signs or hand out leaflets. Says Hepburn, "I learned early what it is to be snubbed for a good cause. Snobbery has never worried me since."

All the Hepburn children were encouraged to think for them-selves, to have and defend their own opinions. They were also urged by their father to participate in all sorts of athletic activities; he thought it was the best way to safeguard their health. Kate learned to figure skate, to swim and dive, to play golf and tennis, even to wrestle and do gymnastics – including the trapeze! In her teens she took up competitive sports and won a medal for figureskating, and even reached the semi-final of a state-wide golf tournament.

The family was really the only social environment that Kate knew. In conservative Hartford, the Hepburns were an oddity. And as a child, Kate was 7 a little too aggressive, a little too sure of herself, to make close friends outside the family. The fact that she was not sent to school but tutored at home for years increased her social isolation. She simply never learned how to get along with her peers.

But she was not lonely nor unhappy because she had her family. Her closest companion was her older brother Tom, by all accounts a lively boy. Tom and Kate went to visit family friends for Easter, 1920, when she was ten and he was sixteen and, as a special treat, they were taken to see a stage production of *A Connecticut Yankee In King Arthur's Court*. They were both fascinated by a scene in which an actor appeared to be hanged and speculated about how he managed to perform the trick safely. The next morning, when Tom failed to come down to breakfast, Kate went looking for him and found him hanging from the attic rafters. Since she was alone in the house, she ran frantically out onto the strange streets calling for help. Eventually, she found a policeman and a doctor who confirmed that Tom had been dead for hours. The loss of her brother, and the mysterious circumstances of his death, cast a shadow on the rest of her childhood.

Katharine Hepburn entered prestigious Bryn Mawr college in 1924, when she was just sixteen. She was a tall angular girl, with uncontrollable red hair that she usually wore in a bun, blue-grey eyes that looked straight at you and a high-pitched penetrating voice. Unused to the social conventions that dominated the lives of most of her classmates, she covered her uncertainty with an air of bravado that won her few friends.

It was at college that she became seriously interested in drama, which gave her a chance to participate in college activities and to attract favorable attention. She had parts in several college productions and in her senior year, she won the part of Pandora in an Elizabethan pastoral called *The Woman In The Moone*. She made a great impression and got lots of applause. Legend has it that she decided then and there to pursue an acting career.

When she graduated in 1928, she obtained from a college friend a letter of introduction to Edwin Knopf, who ran a summer stock company in Baltimore. She remembered her father's dictum: "If you want to get somewhere, don't write a letter. Go over and appear personally. They can throw a letter into the wastepaper basket, but they can't do that to *you*." So she simply turned up at the theatre. Knopf recalls that "She was tremendously sincere but awkward, green and freaky-looking. I wanted no part of her. But it wasn't so easy to get rid of Hepburn." Her persistence finally wore him down and he gave her a bit part, the role of a lady-in-waiting in *The Czarina*. The star, Mary Boland complained that Hepburn stared at her continually and got on her nerves but she eventually fell victim to the Hepburn persistence and took the young actress under her wing, helping her to dress and make up.

Later in the summer, Hepburn had another bit part as a flapper in *The Cradle Snatchers*. When it closed, Knopf told her candidly that her shrill voice was a serious handicap to a career in the theatre. She was already worried because she often lost her voice during a performance so was responsive to the suggestion from stage manager Kenneth McKenna that she work with a voice coach. He recommended Frances Robinson-Duff, who had taught, among others, Helen Hayes and Clark Gable.

Hepburn announced to her family that she planned to go to New York to study for her chosen career in the theatre. They greeted the news with dismay. To them, it was like deciding to join the circus and her father harshly accused her of wanting to show off. No one expected her to succeed.

They reckoned without her determination. Not long after she arrived in New York, she learned that Knopf was going to produce a play on Broadway and she hounded him into giving her the small part of the secretary in *The Big Pond.* In addition, she understudied the leading lady so, when after several weeks, Knopf decided to fire the star, Hepburn got the lead. She worked hard on the part wth her coach and the rehearsals were satisfactory but opening night (out of town, on Long Island) was a fully-fledged disaster. Hepburn had a bad case of nerves. She arrived late at the theatre and then wouldn't go on until she shed her costume's underpants which she said were scratching her. She mixed up her lines, tripped over her own feet and, as she got more distraught, talked faster and faster until no-one, not even the rest of the cast, could understand a word she was saying. She was fired as soon as the curtain went down.

But she didn't give up and landed another small part in a play called *These Days.* The play ran eight nights, and Hepburn was favourably mentioned in several reviews. Not exactly what you'd call a triumph but it led to more work. The same producers then hired her as an understudy for Hope Williams in *Holiday.* The play ran for eight months but unfortunately for Hepburn, the star remained in excellent health and never missed a performance.

Soon after the play opened, Katharine Hepburn surprised everyone – perhaps most of all herself – by getting married. Her groom was Ludlow Ogden Smith, a Philadelphia socialite who was an old friend of the family. They were engaged only a few weeks before the wedding, on December 12, 1928. It was a private ceremony at the Hepburn home in Hartford and afterward the couple departed for a brief honeymoon in Bermuda.

The marriage seems to have been an impulsive escape attempt at normality which Hepburn began to regret almost immediately. Nothing about her married life suited her, not even her name. She drew the line at being called Kate Smith, like the girlishly sentimental popular singer, so her husband agreed to become just Ogden Ludlow. She hated the demands of domesticity. Reading between the lines, one guesses she also disliked the sexual element in what was really a friendship. Most of all, she hated giving up her freedom. She felt an enormous conflict between her ideal of marriage – being a devoted wife whose only interest in life is her husband and family – and the reality of her own intense desire for a career in the theatre.

The couple were so unhappy that they separated after just three weeks of marriage. They remained good friends for years, and often went on holidays together. Garson Kanin later said, "When one sees her with Luddy (as she calls him) it is clear that they share the compassionate interchange of two people who, once, long ago, were in a bad accident together but survived." They were officially divorced in 1934, when Luddy wanted to remarry – with Kate's blessing.

She threw herself back into her acting career, returning to her job 9 as understudy in *Holiday*. Not long after it closed, she got the lead in an Italian fantasy called *Death Takes A Holiday*, produced by Lee Shubert. She was fired during the previews and told about it just before she went on for her final performance. She recently fumed, "I was goddamned upset, and angry too, that they'd fired me just before the curtain went up. How did they know that I wouldn't go mad and not be able to give a performance?" She laughingly adds, "I went back to the hotel and an actor who was in the cast said, 'You can't be alone.' So he read me a play, a terribly bad play that he'd written, and I thought 'I'd rather be alone and weeping than trying to keep awake here.' Being fired was easy compared to that play."

Her next work was understudying the part of Vera in the Theatre Guild production of *A Month In The Country*. In the middle of the run, she replaced the actress who played the bit part of the maid. The director was Reuben Mamoulian, later to go to Hollywood himself, and he remembers the awkward first impression Hepburn made. But he hired her because he noticed about her a luminosity in the way her skin caught the light that made him think she would be a presence.

In the summer of 1930, Frances Robinson-Duff arranged for Hepburn to join a summer stock company in Stockbridge, Massachusetts, along with another of her students, Laura Harding. The two girls immediately became close friends. But the rest of the company was not impressed. Hepburn did get parts in two productions, *A Romantic Young Lady* and *The Admirable Crichton* but she was noticed by her peers chiefly for her eccentricities: her high squeaky voice, her endless baths, her love of practical jokes and her unconventional relationship with her husband. One actor remembers, "Her husband came up every weekend and she promptly sent him off to the village for a quart of ice cream. He washed her hair in the tub, and that, and fetching the ice cream, was about all he did that weekend, as far as she was concerned." Hepburn did not flourish in the chummy social environment of the summer stock company and she was annoyed that she didn't get more and better parts. She left midway through the season.

The next fall, she landed another Broadway part, playing Jane Cowl's daughter in something called *Art And Mrs. Bottle*. The playwright hated her, declaring, "She looks a fright, her manner is objectionable, and she has no talent," and so she was soon fired. They tried fourteen other actresses in the part and eventually returned to Hepburn. When the production finally opened, she drew praise from many critics but the play did not run very long.

She did another season of summer stock in 1931, this time in Ivoryton, Connecticut. In the fall, she was offered a good part in Philip Barry's new play, *The Animal Kingdom* but the star and co-producer Leslie Howard detested her mannerisms (and possibly also her height) and she was fired after a week. When she called Barry to protest, he replied, "Nobody who has your disposition could ever play light comedy. I'm glad they fired you."

Much later, she told biographer Charles Higham, "I was always geting fired. I was what might be called a 'flash actor.' I could read a part without knowing what I was doing better than anyone in the whole world. I could laugh and cry, and I could always get a part quickly – but I couldn't keep it! They got on to me after a while. I would lose my voice, fall down on lines, get red in the face, talk too fast and I couldn't act. The sight of people out there just petrified me!''

It speaks volumes for Hepburn's persistence and determination that she never gave up despite all these debacles. It also speaks for her talent that somehow she always found another part. Her next one was the female lead in *The Warrior's Husband,* a play by Julian Thompson loosely based on the Greek classic *Lysistrata.* Hepburns played Antiope, Queen of the Amazons, a brash warrior who is eventually tamed and made womanly by love.

The part was perfect for her. It displayed all her energy and verve (and in the short Amazonian costume, her very attractive legs as well.) It used her athleticism to great advantage – what other dramatic actress could make an entrance carrying a huge stuffed deer as she leapt lithely down a flight of stairs? Stage manager Phyllis Seaton reminisces, ''I'll never forget opening night. The audience was *amazed* by Kate. Her beauty shone through her face. Her skin was transparent, alight with colour and health. Her red hair *blazed* around her face. She had terrific grace . . . she *jumped* at the audience. The audience responded to her immediately. This was a star! You could smell it, you could feel it. It was all around you – the perfume of success!''

The play was a turning point for Hepburn and through a chain of circumstances, it brought her to the attention of David Selznick, head of RKO. When her new agent, Leland Hayward, told her of the studio's interest, Hepburn responded by telling him to ask for $1500 a week. (On Broadway, she was lucky to make $100.) If she was going to sell out to Hollywood, she was at least going to get a good price for it! Perhaps she was more surprised than anyone else when Selznick wired back, ''OK, if her test's good.''

The test was for the part of Syndey Fairfield in *A Bill Of Divorcement,* playing the daughter of John Barrymore. Ten years earlier, the stage version had made a star of Katharine Cornell; now Hollywood was looking for the right girl to repeat the magic. A lot of actresses had tested – including Norma Shearer and Irene Dunne but so far, no magic. Hepburn recalls, ''When I got a chance to test, I looked at the scene and I thought, 'Well, hell, no wonder – the scene's no good.' So I made some excuse and said I couldn't do that scene for the test, but would they let me do a scene of my own?''

The studio agreed and so she tested with a scene from *Holiday.* She got her friend Alan Campbell to do the scene with her but astutely had the whole scene shot over his shoulder (''I didn't want that nonsense about the one helping with the test getting the job'') so she was the centre of interest every second. She said, ''I could imagine what it was like sitting in a projection room watching one girl after another play the same scene, over and over again. Finally, they get so immune to the scene it doesn't have any meaning. So when I came on, looking sort of strange and mysterious, they heard a new scene – and it worked.'' She thought at the time she was projecting control and nonchalance; however, when she saw the test later, she recalls thinking, ''It was obviously the test of someone who was totally panicked. It was heartbreaking in its eagerness to please.''

Director George Cukor still remembers the effect of that test. He    11

says, "There was this odd creature; she wasn't strictly speaking 'pretty.' I watched her in the sequence from *Holiday,* and I wasn't knocked sideway. I didn't say, the way they do in pictures, 'Aaahh, great!' It doesn't happen that way. Instead you use little indications, things that might be promising." For Cukor, the indication was the way she picked up a glass. "The camera focused on her back. There was an *enormous* feeling, a *weight* about the manner in which she picked up the glass. I thought she was very talented in that action." Apparently, that little sign of talent was all Cukor required because she was offered her contract at $1500 a week and the part of Sydney for her screen debut.

On July 1, 1932, Hepburn and her good friend Laura Harding boarded the train for the four-day trip to California. Her arrival in Pasadena three days later was anything but auspicious. Somewhere west of Albuquerque, Hepburn had stuck her head out the train window to gaze at some particularly scenic view and had got a cinder in her eye, which immediately swelled shut. She was wearing a silk suit that she had thought smart but which somehow struck Californians as ludicrous. She was rumpled, her hair was messy, she could barely see and the pain in her eye was distracting. She was met in this condition at the station by her agent Hayward and his partner Myron Selznick, David's brother. As he caught sight of her standing bedraggled on the platform, Selznick asked Hayward, in a voice perfectly audible to Hepburn, "My God, Leland, is this what we're sticking David fifteen hundred a week for?"

14

*Bill Of Divorcement* was Hepburn's first film – in this scene with Elizabeth Patterson as her mother.

# 2

# The First Year in Hollywood

*Shooting on Hepburn's first picture, A Bill Of Divorcement,* started on July 9, 1932, just five days after she arrived in Hollywood. The movie was finished one month later and released in September.

Hepburn's screen debut was in the very sympathetic role of Sydney Fairfield who lives with her mother (Billie Burke). Her father (John Barrymore) has been in an asylum for years, suffering from hereditary insanity made worse by shell-shock in the First World War. On the very day that his divorced wife is to remarry, Hillary Fairfield escapes from the asylum and turns up on their doorstep. Although he is upset when he learns he is losing his wife, he eventually pulls himself together and lets her go gracefully as a proof of his love for her. Meanwhile Sydney, shocked by her father's insanity, decides it would be unwise to marry and have children who might also be afflicted, so she nobly sends away her own fiancé. She remains with her father, devoting herself to his care.

The director of *A Bill Of Divorcement* was George Cukor, himself still a relative newcomer to Hollywood. Cukor is often called a "woman's director" because he has coaxed great performances out of his leading ladies and Hepburn benefited from working with someone so sympathetic and supportive. Perhaps part of Cukor's genius is simply his willingness to stick with his star through her weaknesses as well as her strengths, giving the audience time to know and accept her.

Certainly, Hepburn's performance in *A Bill Of Divorcement* is uneven. In many of the scenes, especially early in the picture, she is visibly awkward, edgy, unsure of herself. Her voice is high and shrill, always a sign of her unease. But despite – or possibly because of – these weaknesses, she made a real impact.

Cukor believes he can pinpoint the very moment in the film when Hepburn became a star. "There was an interesting moment in the picture where they have first seen her, and she spoke rather forcefully, and the audience wasn't quite sure whether they liked her or not. And then there was, mercifully, an interval where she said goodbye to her mother, who was troubled. And you saw this girl go to the door and she smiled. And you saw that she had this lovely smile. And the audience had time to take stock of her when she walked across this big room and took the cushion . . . and lay on the hearthstone, and then they could see that she moved beautifully and she had a lovely figure, and there was a nice interval to take stock to her. And it was at that moment that Katharine Hepburn became a star."

Hepburn was especially effective in the scenes she played opposite Barrymore. She gives the veteran actor much of the credit: "He just shoved me into what I ought to do before the camera. He taught me all that he could pour into one greenhorn in that short time." Cukor agrees. "Barrymore instructed her and made things very easy and pleasant for her."

But the friendly relationship between the stars ended abruptly. Barrymore told Garson Kanin about it several years later. He said that after the first few days on the set, "I gave her the eye a few times. Then I stopped till she gave me the eye. After a few more days, we gave each other the eye. So I knew the time was ready." According to him, "Several days later, we went over to my dressing room. I locked the door and took my clothes off. She just stood there looking at me and finally I said, 'Well, come on, what are you waiting for? We don't have all day.' She didn't move, so I did and started to grab her but she backed away and practically plastered herself against the wall. I said, 'What's the matter?' And she said, 'I *cahn't*!' I said, 'Never mind, I'll show you how.' She started babbling, 'No, no. Please. It's impossible. I *cahn't*.' I've never been so damned flabbergasted. I said to her, 'Why not?' And what do you think she said? 'My father doesn't want me to have any babies!'"

Hepburn concurs with the general outline of the story, although she denies that she ever gave Barrymore cause to leap to the conclusion that she was interested. Her unsophisticated response is oddly revealing and it also suggests some of the reasons she needed to adopt a brusquely protective manner. Whatever really happened, Barrymore was furious about being rejected and rarely spoke to her thereafter.

*A Bill Of Divorcement* was a moderately successful movie but it made Hepburn a star when it opened in September. She celebrated with a brief trip to Europe (with Luddy for a companion) and the press were waiting for her when she returned, a sure sign of success. RKO picked up her option and she settled down in a little rented house with Laura to keep her company. Defiantly, she refused to play the Hollywood game. She wouldn't give interviews, she wouldn't pretend to be in love with her leading men and she wouldn't even go to the parties where stars "must" be seen. Part of this haughty attitude may have come from Broadway's disdain for Hollywood but much of it was probably due to her feelings of insecurity, the sense of being an outsider in a tight little

*Christopher Strong* – as Lady Cynthia in fancy dress costume.

company town. Underneath the show of unconcern was a continuing determination to succeed.

Hepburn's second film was *Christopher Strong* which started shooting in the late fall of 1932. This time she was the star. She played the part of Lady Cynthia Darrington, a romantic combination of society beauty and aviatrix (the word itself is a wonderful clue to the attitudes of the times). Lady Cynthia falls in love with a married politician, played by Colin Clive and they have a brief passionate idyll. The lovers try to separate both for the sake of his wife (Billie Burke) and his career but they are unable to stay apart. Then Lady Cynthia discovers she is pregnant. She finds her own way out in the final scene, when she first sets the world altitude record by soaring to 30,000 feet and then rips off her oxygen mask to die free and alone in the clouds.

Obviously the plot itself is hokey. But Zoe Akins, who adapted the novel for the screen, provided a few good strong scenes and Dorothy Arzner, a pioneering woman director, made the most of them. Arzner and Hepburn did not get along well and work on the film was made tense by their conflicts. They had very different styles and they were both strong women determined to make it on their own terms. But despite their lack of personal harmony, Arzner had all the right instincts about the way to present Katharine Hepburn and *Christopher Strong*, although it was not a box office success, in many ways set the pattern for the Hepburn screen persona.

First there was the nobility of character. Hepburn always played a woman of great integrity willing to sacrifice everything, even her own life, for her principles. Another element was the defiance of social convention: the Hepburn character was moral but it was not society's rules that she followed.

A third aspect was an emphasis on the unusualness of her looks. In her first movie, make-up men had tried to make her conform to the Hollywood norm of femininity by covering up her freckles and painting on a cupid's-bow mouth; her costumes were the conventional dresses that a well-brought-up girl would wear. Arzner had the wit to let Hepburn wear pants, a beret pulled down squarely over her hair and a most masculine aviator's cap. These slightly outré clothes made Hepburn stand out and gave her an air of distinction. Most memorable of all was the costume (for a fancy dress party that Lady Cynthia attends) that was made entirely out of metal and included a skull-hugging cap with little moth antennae. This bizarre outfit was wretchedly uncomfortable. Hepburn had to stand all the time she was wearing it (it didn't bend), the metal scraped her skin if she took a deep breath and it was so heavy it made her sick. But it was enormously effective; it made her look like a creature from another planet when she was on the screen with the other society girls in their frilly little dresses.

Arzner was also the first to discover that Hepburn was most successful on the screen when she was forced to underplay. The discovery came in a key scene, a conversation between the two lovers about their feelings. Arzner was troubled by Hepburn's overacting when she pressed too hard and made her speech too dramatic to be believable. Arzner said she "finally decided that it had to be two people just looking dead ahead, two people who couldn't express any emotion – just a monotonous emptiness. At first she (Hepburn) played the scene headlong but when I told her to look blank, she did, and her voice went wonderfully flat and toneless. She and Colin Clive played it superbly – people said it was the best love story on the screen." It took Hepburn many more years to master her tendency to overact and her early films are frequently marred by too much attitudinizing, too much conscious projection and too many stage histrionics for the intimacy of film.

Although *Christopher Strong* was not a box-office success, the reviews for Hepburn were good. By midwinter of 1933, just six months after she had arrived in Hollywood, she was set for her third picture. *Morning Glory* was an original work of Zoe Akins (since Akins' husband died during the preparation of the script, scenarist Howard Green was called in to do the final polishing.) Dorothy Arzner had planned to direct the picture but she lost interest after the difficulties of working with Hepburn on *Christopher Strong* and so producer Pandro Berman took it over as a personal project.

Hepburn remembers her first sight of the script. It was before the project had even been mentioned to her. She was waiting for Berman in his office, saw the script on his desk and idly picked it up. She says, "I thought, oh my God, that's the most wonderful part ever written for anyone." So she stole the script and went away to read it. A few hours later, she reappeared in Berman's office, apologized for being late and told him why. Then she asked to do *Morning Glory*. He told her that it was intended as a vehicle for Constance Bennett but Hepburn pleaded it should be hers and Berman gave in. There is evidence from other sources that the crafty Berman set up the entire scenario simply to hook Hepburn, whom he had intended all along for the part. If it was a ploy, it certainly worked beautifully.

For Hepburn, the part in *Morning Glory* was worthy of all these schemes. She played Eva Lovelace, a young actress from Vermont who comes to New York to seek her fame and fortune on Broadway. Her determination to succeed wins the respect of a veteran actor (C. Aubrey Smith) and he takes her to a fancy party given in honour of the well-known star, Rita Vernon. At the party, Eva gets drunk on champagne and ends up giving all the Broadway luminaries an example of her own ideas about acting in a very unusual rendition of Juliet's balcony scene. Because of the sensation created by her outburst, she meets a suave manager, played by Adolphe Menjou. They have a brief affair but true love is lurking in the wings, in the shape of an up-and-coming young playwright (Douglas Fairbanks, Jr.). His play goes to Broadway with Rita Vernon in the lead but the temperamental star walks out on opening night. Of course Eva knows the script by heart, goes on in her place and a star is born.

The basic plot of *Morning Glory* was already an old chestnut in 1933. But the part of Eva was exactly right for Katharine Hepburn – especially since there was more than a little of Eva in her own personality. She gave the role depth from her own experiences of struggling for attention, supported only by her own almost obsessive belief in her own talent. She was able to bring out Eva's stubborn determination, as well as the little touch of craziness latent in such a display of unsupported self-belief.

To direct, Berman selected Lowell Sherman, who tried an approach unusual in Hollywood. He spent a week with the cast, rehearsing their

*Morning Glory* – Hepburn won the 1933 Academy Award for Best Actress in her role as Eva Lovelace. Her co-star was Douglas Fairbanks, Jr.

parts and discussing their characters then he shot the picture straight through, taking only eighteen days. This method of working, so unlike the usual Hollywood system of shooting scenes in almost random sequence, was particularly beneficial to Hepburn with her stage training and no doubt helped her give her best performance.

Again, the reviews for Hepburn were better than the reviews for the movie. Today, *Morning Glory* is rarely shown even in revival houses for the creaking plot and the general overacting make it a tedious experience. Hepburn's balcony scene is embarrassing – such simpering you've never witnessed and the romantic hero is a wimp, a fact which undermines the credibility of the love scenes. But some of Hepburn's moments are still affecting. A contemporary review in *Time* said, "From this immemorial fairy tale, the delicate muscled face of heroine Hepburn shines out like a face on a coin. Of the brash little provincial she makes a strangely distinguished character, a little mad from hunger and dreams, absurdly audacious and trusting." One person who is still impressed is the Hepburn of today. "My brother-in-law had a print and I said, 'Well, that's old enough for me to look at. I can't even remember that person.' Watching it, I was absolutely fascinated. I thought, 'My God, not bad at all. What one does learn?'"

Some months after *Morning Glory* was released, Katharine Hepburn was nominated for the 1933 Academy Award as Best Actress. Her competition was May Robson for *Lady For A Day* and Diana Wynward for *Cavalcade*. Hepburn assumed she had no chance against two such veterans and gave the matter no more thought; in fact, she embarked on a trip to Paris the day of the presentation in March, 1934. But much to her surprise, she was the winner. It was a great triumph for so young an actress, in the early stages of her career.

Within weeks of finishing *Morning Glory* in the spring of 1933, Hepburn was already immersed in her next project – *Little Women*. David Selznick had wanted to film the book for years and finally he assembled what he thought was the right team. The script was by Victor Heerman and his wife Sarah Mason who had resolutely tried to avoid sentimentality and stick to the underlying gritty story of a New England family trying to keep going during the crisis of wartime. George Cukor was hired to direct. He had never read the novel before (Hepburn fondly claims she doesn't believe he ever finished it) and remembers his reaction: "I was absolutely startled because it had all the American virtues – duty, love of family, love of parents, respect for parents, hard work, all the staples that I think are admirable."

Cukor agreed with Selznick and the Heermans that the film should be realistic rather than romantic, down-to-earth and not slick. He hired an art director to reproduce the simple house in Concord, Massachusetts, where author Louisa May Alcott grew up. He instructed Walter Plunkett, the costume designer, to make the clothes out of homely and worn materials – the sort of dresses the real Alcott girls would have worn. (As an additional touch of realism, Plunkett had them trade their clothes back and forth.)

Cukor wanted Hepburn for the part of tom-boyish Jo, who struggles to achieve independence as a writer and a woman. Cukor said, "Kate was born for the part of Jo. She's tender and odd and funny, sweet and yet tough, intensely loyal, with an enormous sense of family and all of Jo's burning

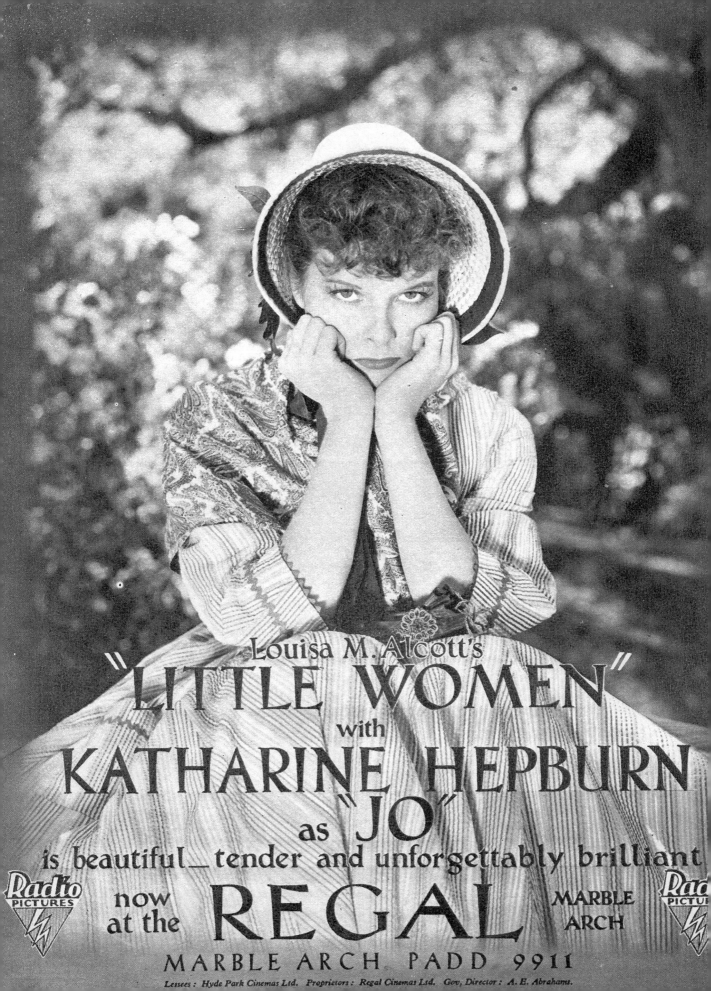

ambition and at heart a pure clean simplicity and firmness.'' *Little Women* was the second of the many films Cukor and Hepburn did together and one of the most successful.

In case you've managed to forget the plot of *Little Women,* Jo is one of the four March sisters growing up in a little town in Massachusetts during the Civil War. Her father is away fighting and her mother (Spring Byington) is trying her best to manage without him. Jo is the second daughter, the stubborn and headstrong one. She opposes the marriage of older sister Meg (Frances Dee) and her bitter feelings about this event lead her to turn down a proposal from her childhood sweetheart, Laurie, played by Douglass Montgomery. Then Jo leaves for New York, to learn to be a writer and make her own way in the world. There she meets the scholarly Professor Bhaer (Paul Lukas) who encourages her in her career and will by the end of the film become her husband. Meanwhile, back at the homefront, Jo's younger sister Amy (played by the recently married Joan Bennett, who was growing visibly more pregnant every day) falls in love with Laurie and they marry. Jo comes home again when the youngest girl, the delicate Beth (Jean Parker) is dying. The story ends when Mr. March returns from the war, and the family (Jo has the professor in tow by this pont) is reunited at last.

The whole picture was executed with taste and care and it was nominated for Best Picture of 1934. Cukor was nominated for Best Director but the only Academy Award it actually won was for the Heermans' screenplay. *Little Women* had good casting and good ensemble playing but the star of the picture was certainly Katharine Hepburn. Even when she started to speak to her dead sister ''up there in the sky'', Hepburn was convincing. Cukor later said, ''Kate Hepburn had cast a spell of magic and a kind of power over the picture. You could go with whatever she did. She really felt it all very deeply. She's a New England girl who understands all that and has her own family feeling.''

That was a good year for Katharine Hepburn. *Little Women,* her fourth picture in the first year of her movie career, was a big financial success. With the Oscar for *Morning Glory,* and the good reviews for the other pictures, her future seemed assured.

Yet in only a few years – after a string of roles that were artistic failures, financial flops or both – she was publicly labelled ''Box Office Poison'' and so unemployable that she was forced to leave Hollywood.

*Little Women* – from Film Weekly, January 26th, 1934.

A publicity shot taken during the shooting of *Spitfire*

# 3

## Box Office Poison

*How do you reward an* actress who's just been nominated for an Academy Award and acclaimed in a big box office success? Apparently you give her the role of Trigger, a hillbilly tom-boy faith healer, in an absurdity called *Spitfire*. It was a picture that took four weeks to film and less time to forget. Contemporary reviews were surprisingly kind to the spectacle of Katharine Hepburn impersonating a girlish hermit of the Ozarks (complete with execrable accent and bare feet.) The *New Yorker,* for example, said gently, ''Her artistry does not extend to the intepretation of the primitive or the uncouth.''

Hepburn fans claim she accepted the role only because it was part of a deal with RKO to let her take time off afterward. On the other hand, there are Hepburn critics who insist she rather fancied herself in the part of the rural mystic. The director, John Cromwell, takes this point of view, explaining, ''She had all the self-confidence in the world . . . so much so that I doubt that even for a moment did she ever think there was anything she couldn't do.'' Whatever the reason for her appearance as Trigger, it did her career no good.

When her work in *Spitfire* was finished, Hepburn left for New York and rehearsals for a play. Some months earlier, she had been approached by producer Jed Harris who was fresh from a string of stage successes and acclaimed the wonder of Broadway. He wanted her to take a supporting role in a play that starred Laurence Olivier but she felt she was ready to carry a production herself. Harris realized that her film stardom would bring customers into the theatre so he looked for a vehicle. What he found was *The Lake,* a play that had been a modest success in London a few years earlier.

Things started off badly and never got better. Harris later said, 25

"From that moment of decision (to do the play) I hated myself. It's the only time in my whole life in the theatre I ever ventured into 'show business', which is all that *The Lake* with Katharine Hepburn amounted to." Hepburn herself admits, "I knew almost right away I was wrong for that damned part."

During the three weeks of rehearsal, Harris, who had something of a reputation for his difficult behaviour toward actors, treated Hepburn savagely. She responded, as she always did when she felt threatened, with an air of haughty unconcern. But whatever her pose, she badly needed a supportive director who would not only help her work out her part but also bolster her self-confidence about her return to the stage. Instead, she got an angry man who was outraged by her defences and tried to pull them down.

The play previewed in Washington and everyone knew it wasn't working. But the publicity had been all too successful, creating a wave of expectation and advance ticket sales of $40,000. So despite everyone's trepidations, *The Lake* opened on Broadway the day after Christmas, 1933. Dorothy Parker's comment was the most famous: "Katharine Hepburn ran the gamut of emotions from A to B." Other reviews were less malicious but no less harsh. Hepburn recalls, "On opening night I was simply petrified. My voice went all loony and I must have been stiff as a board. I'm sure my performance was foul."

Unfortunately, there was no easy way out of this humiliating situation. Despite the terrible reviews, the advance tickets sales kept *The Lake* open. So for fifty four more nights, Hepburn had to play in front of an audience that she could only assume had come to see her make a fool of herself. Finally, she asked Harris to close the show – a privilege for which he made her pay $15,000. She went home to Hartford to try to recover her equilibrium.

In the summer of 1934, she was back in Hollywood, working under a new contract ($300,000 for six films) at RKO. They had decided that the success of *Little Women* indicated she should appear in costume dramas, so they cast her as Lady Babbie, the quaintly charming heroine of *The Little Minister*. Hepburn has said, "I really didn't want to play it until I heard another actress was desperate for the role. Then, of course, it became the most importan thing in the world for me that I should get it." Perhaps it's no coincidence that the other actress was Margaret Sullavan, who also happened to be the other woman in the life of Leland Hayward, Hepburn's agent, with whom she had recently become personally involved.

Although the screenplay (based on the novel and play by James M. Barrie) was written by Victor Heerman and Sarah Mason, it was a far-from-ideal part for Katharine Hepburn – or any other actress. Lady Babbie is the high-born ward of a powerful lord but she prefers to dress up as a gypsy and mingle with the poor weavers who are planning to rebel against her guardian. While thus disguised, she meets the local minister (John Beal) and they fall in love. The scandal of this courtship causes the church elders to take steps to expel the minister from their church. But then Lady Babbie's true identity is revealed and all is forgiven.

The plot is preposterous – and unpleasantly snobby – and the part of Lady Babbie is too whimsical to be palatable. Although the play (which originally starred Maude Adams, an actress much admired by Hepburn) had been a success, its light whimsy did not translate into the medium of film. The director, Richard Wallace, failed to take a strong enough hand with his actors, preferring to let them work out their own characterizations and Hepburn seems to have chosen to model her performance on that of Maude Adams but since she was an altogether different type, the imitation was not felicitous.

Still, the critics continued to be tolerant. Eileen Creelman said, "Miss Hepburn, gauntly handsome and spirited, makes no attempt to become that elusive charming creature, a Barrie heroine. She is just Miss Hepburn, arch, vivid, varying little, adored by a vast public." Unfortunately, adoring or not, the vast public was not willing to sit through Katharine Hepburn in a Scottish accent being elfin.

What Hepburn needed was a good movie. What she got was *Break Of Hearts.* The best you can say about it is that at least she didn't have an accent. Hepburn played the part of Constance Dane, a young struggling composer. She falls in love with a famous conductor but puts an end to the affair when she discovers he is seeing another woman. She meets a nice young man who wants marry her but she abandons him when she learns that the conductor is drinking so heavily his career and health are endangered. Convinced that only she can save him, she returns to his side.

John Barrymore was originally slated to play the hero, but he was otherwise engaged (as someone wittily put it, he must have seen the script.) Then the part was given to Francis Lederer, a Czech stage actor. Hepburn thought he was all wrong for the part and the assistant director didn't like his insistence on showing only his good profile. So he was replaced by Charles Boyer.

Despite good efforts from Hepburn and Boyer, the film was a failure. Some critics blame the director, Philip Moeller and others blame the script, once again by the Heermans. Whatever the reasons, audiences stayed away in droves and critics were caustic. *Time* said that "Charles Boyer manages to make the defeat he receives from his material comparatively graceful"; as for Hepburn, "she makes it clear that unless her employers see fit to restore her to roles in keeping with her mannerisms, these will presently annoy cinemaddicts into forgetting that she is really an actress of great promise and considerable style."

Both RKO and Hepburn were getting discouraged. Pandro Berman, who had produced most of her films, later commented, "By this time I realized Kate wasn't a movie star. She wasn't going to become a star either, in the sense that Crawford or Shearer were – actresses able to drag an audience in by their own efforts. She was a hit only in hit pictures; she couldn't save a flop. And she almost invariably chose the wrong vehicles."

But Berman found the right vehicle, for a change. It was *Alice Adams,* based on the novel by Booth Tarkington. The heroine is, as Walter Kerr put it, "a lower-middle-class girl of better-than-that pretensions . . . She is pushy, she is willing to lie about her family social standing, she is – to her knowing neighbours – the town joke." But Alice is smart enough to know she's a counterfeit and spirited enough to want to be the real thing; she is ultimately a sympathetic heroine. Hepburn loved playing Alice. The film's director, George

*Sylvia Scarlett* – Hepburn in the title role dressed as a boy.

Stevens, has said, "Kate impressed me deeply with her effort to reach out to the role. She was the opposite of Alice Adams; she was a privileged woman, born to money. She was forceful, vividly expressive, strong, even strident and now she had to be subdued, restrained, perhaps beaten by life in a way Kate never could have been." Stevens' challenge was to help her learn to act the part. He succeeded so well that many people believe Alice Adams is Hepburn's best performance.

The plot is simple, revolving around the various attempts of members of the Adams family to improve their social status. Mr. Adams (Fred Stone), prodded by his wife, is trying to find backing for his own little business whereas the son (Frank Albertson), takes a shortcut and steals money from his employer. Alice meets and falls for a young engineer (Fred MacMurray) and hopes to marry her way but the failure of her pretension to an appropriate social background makes her despair and she enrolls in a secretarial course. There is a happy ending: the son is forgiven, the father gets the backing he needs and girl gets boy (an ending quite unlike the more realistic conclusion of the novel).

The production was RKO at its best: script largely by Mortimer Offner, costumes by Walter Plunkett, art direction by Van Nest Polglase. There were inspired comic performances from Grady Sutton as Alice's pompous dancing partner and Hattie McDaniel as an incompetent maid. Stevens directed with a sure sense of what was wanted and a willingness to demand it from his star. He put one scene, with Hepburn chatting to MacMurray on her front porch, through more than eighty takes before he wore her down and got her to do it his way. Another scene that provoked a stormy confrontation between director and star was one in which Stevens wanted her to go to a window in her bedroom and begin to cry (the scene would be shot from outside the window, showing both the rain and her tears.) Hepburn was embarrassed to cry "in front of millions of people," but Stevens berated her for her selfishness. He said, "I feel for all those Alice Adams girls who are watching this, who are going to know something about this kind of pain . . . The girls are going to be sitting there at the Music Hall, and they want themselves to be up there, not a rich movie actress." As you know if you've seen the movie, Stevens won — and he was right.

Perhaps the most memorable scene in the movie is the dance Alice attends. Hepburn's portrayal of a wallflower is a painful classic. We laugh at her homemade dress, her awkwardness, her absolutely transparent attempts to appear amused and at her ease. But we also feel the dreadful humiliation of Alice's social isolation and admire the bravery of spirit that gets her through such a nightmare.

When the picture was released in August, 1935, the reviews were good and a few months later, Hepburn received her second nomination for an Academy Award (she lost to Bette Davis). The film was a modest box office success at the time; it has since become a staple of revival houses.

Encouraged by this step in the right direction, Berman went on to make a real blunder: he allowed Hepburn to choose her own next picture. She got together with George Cukor and came up with Sylvia Scarlett, based on the Compton MacKenzie novel. An excellent cast and crew put in a lot of devotion and hard work and came up with . . . a real bomb.

29

Insofar as there is a plot, it is simple. Sylvia Scarlett and her father (Edmund Gwenn) must flee England because he is wanted for larceny; to help them escape detection, Sylvia masquerades as a boy. They join up with a petty crook (Cary Grant playing a Cockney) and have a lot of picaresque adventures on the road. When they meet a wealthy artist, Michael Fane (Brian Aherne) Sylvia falls in love. In order to save him from the competition, a Russian adventuress (Natalie Paley), she resumes her true gender.

Audiences were not ready to see Katharine Hepburn as a boy and they were made uneasy and perhaps disapproving by the sexual ambiguity. Everyone connected with the picture remembers the joy they had in making it but that was the only happiness anyone got out of it for a long time. The reviews were harsh and the fans made themselves scarce. The film lost over $200,000 which is nothing in current terms of disasters like *Heaven's Gate* but then it was considered sizeable. Berman says it was the worst film he ever made and the greatest mistake of Hepburn's career. On the night of the review he was in a rage against both Hepburn and Cukor. They told him they felt guilty about the losses the studio would suffer from backing their hunch and offered to do another picture for nothing. Berman leapt up, shouted, "Oh, God, no! I never want to see either of you again," and stomped off. Interestingly, *Sylvia Scarlett* has recently become something of an underground classic and Cukor says now that his only regret was his decision to tack on a conventional beginning and ending to try to meet the audiences half-way.

Berman of course got over his anger and soon acquired another property for his star: Maxwell Anderson's play *Mary Of Scotland.* It had just closed on Broadway (Helen Hayes played Mary) and Berman believed it would be a good role for Hepburn. The screenplay was written by Dudley Nichols who tried to drop the tedious blank verse and tighten up the action. Perhaps in the hope of further tightening, Berman chose John Ford to direct.

The plot is long and involved and more or less follows the historical facts. It opens with Mary returning to Scotland and marrying Darnley (Douglas Walton). Her secretary Rizzio (John Carradine) is murdered in her very presence and after Darnley has betrayed her to her enemies then he too is slain. Mary next becomes the wife of the Earl of Bothwell (Fredric March) but he is not powerful enough to protect her and is himself exiled. Mary is imprisoned by the Scottish nobles and then, in a purely fictitious scene, she escapes to England to meet with Queen Elizabeth (Florence Eldridge) to ask for help. The result is more long years in prison and, eventually, execution.

John Ford did his best to heighten the drama and inject some action: galloping horses, dark castles with dramatic staircases, glittering daggers and clanking swords. Everyone agreed that Hepburn acquitted herself well in the role of Mary (although there was a certain amount of carping about her accent again) but somehow the film never came to life. Perhaps the material was too historical; perhaps there were not enough strong scenes that revolved around human feelings; perhaps Ford's attempts to turn it into an action-packed epic worked against the nature of Anderson's drama.

Reviewers were polite. Richard Watts said "Hepburn provides a lovely and touching characterization of Mary." Otis Ferguson said she "has and

(Opposite) The front cover of *Picture Show*, June 27th, 1936.

Picture Show, Vol. 35, No. 895. June 27th, 1936. Registered at the G.P.O. as a News

Katharine Hepburn & Brian Aherne in "SYLVIA SCARLETT"

# PICTURE SHOW

THE FILM STAR WEEKLY

**2ᵈ** EVERY FRIDAY

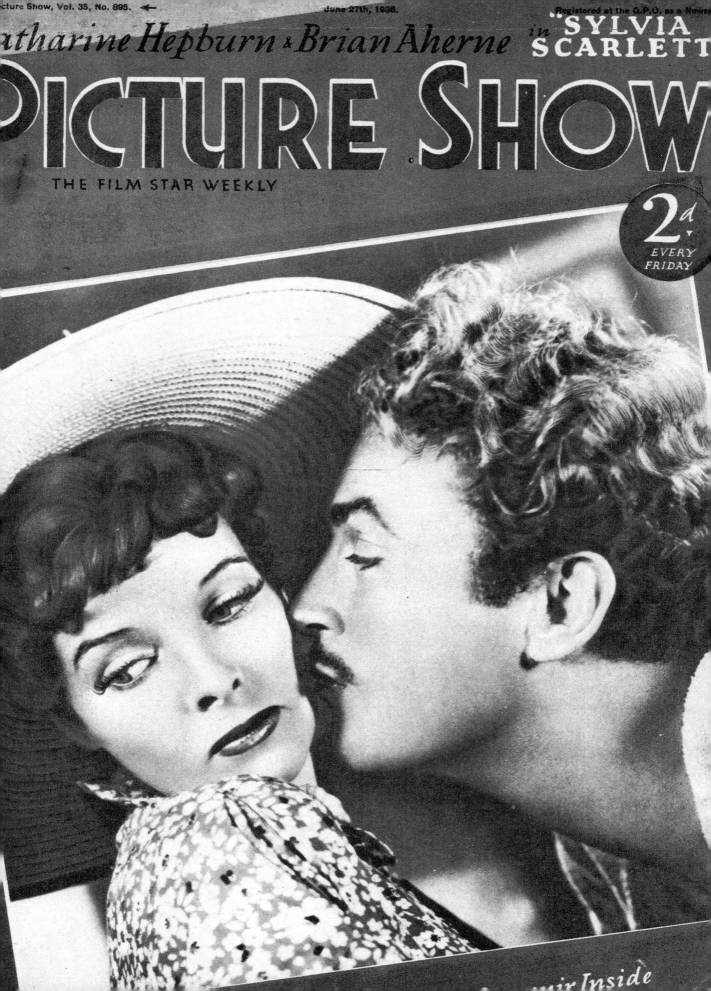

32

The centre spread from Picture Show, June 27th, 1936.

projects over to her audience a high measure of spirit" and that "this screen is made bright and deep for us with the life of a character." The picture's revenues were respectable but not thrilling; *Mary Of Scotland* did not compensate for the disaster of *Sylvia Scarlett*.

Hepburn's next film, *A Woman Rebels,* was another step on the downward path. It did have beautiful costumes by Walter Plunkett (22 of them to be exact), a lovely ballroom sequence by Hermes Pan and the look of historical accuracy, thanks to Van Nest Polglase's art direction. That is the end of the film's catalogue of virtues.

The plot was turgid. Hepburn played Pamela Thistlewaite, a Victorian girl who rebels against the conventions of her time. She has an affair (the lover is played by Van Heflin) and then refuses to marry her faithful suitor Thomas Lane (Herbert Marshall). She goes to work and becomes the editor of a magazine crusading for women's rights but eventually she realizes she really does love the ever-faithful Lane and marries him, presumably to live happily ever after.

It was a feminist message picture of a sort but the pace is slow and the characters bloodless. It was badly received. *Time* said snidely, "Ever since Katharine Hepburn set the cinema industry by the ears with *Little Women,* her employers have been doggedly trying to discover just what elusive factor, added to the stock formula of Lavendar and Old Lace, made the picture so sensationally successful. *A Woman Rebels* represents an effort to discover if the element was the revolt of a young girl against convention. That the experiment is conducted with painstaking care only makes it the more apparent that the hypothesis is faulty."

From Pamela Thistlewaite, Hepburn moved on to Phoebe Throssel; the names alone make you understand why these pictures were such duds. George Stevens directed this James M. Barrie tale of a woman whose suitor (Franchot Tone) goes off to war for ten years. When he returns, she has turned into an old-maid schoolteacher and he doesn't even recognize her. For obscure reasons, she chooses to solve this problem by getting herself up as a fictitious niece, with whom he (along with a number of rivals) falls in love. At the end, she 'Reveals All' and the lover of course immediately proposes.

Again, the Plunkett costumes were the best part of the film but no amount of tasteful embroidery could save this one. The *New York Times* was acerbic: "Hepburn's Phoebe Throssel needs a neurologist far more than a husband. Such flutterings and jitterings and twitchings, such hand-wringings and mouth-quiverings, such runnings about and eyebrow-raising have not been seen on a screen in many a moon."

*Quality Street* was shot in the fall of 1936 as the last film in the RKO contract. Hepburn's future seemed in doubt. *Variety* put it succinctly. "A succession of unfortunate selections of material has marooned a competent girl in a bog of box office frustration. There is probably no one in pictures who needs a real money film as much as this actress." Not long after *Quality Street* was released in 1937, the president of the Independent Theater Owners of America took out a full page ad urging studios to reconsider their constant use of stars who were unable to fill a movie house. He labelled Hepburn (among others) "Box Office Poison." An antidote, however, was just around the corner.    33

*Stage Door.*

# 4

## The Emerging Comedienne

*Hepburn's thoughts turned once again* to the theatre. She still longed for a real success on stage and a Broadway hit might be just the tonic her sagging career needed. She went to the Theatre Guild, managed by a trio of friends – Theresa Helburn, Lawrence Langner and his wife Armina Marshall. Together they came up with the idea of doing a stage adaptation of *Jane Eyre*. The script was written by Helen Jerome, who had just turned out a very successful adaptation of *Pride And Prejudice*. Worthington Miner was chosen to direct. Unfortunately, they had great trouble casting the part of Rochester and ended up with a relatively unknown actor who was unable to hold the stage against Hepburn. *Jane Eyre* opened in New Haven on December 26, 1936 and then moved on to Boston, Chicago and Washington. Hepburn's notices were good but the play itself was weak and Helen Jerome was not enthusiastic about rewriting.

*Jane Eyre*'s good box office business on the road was due in part to Hepburn's celebrity – and the fact that she had become involved in a romance that was the staple of gossip columns. Her personal relationship with Leland Hayward had come to an end about the time she was filming *Quality Street* when he finally married Margaret Sullavan (although he remained her agent as long as he was in the business.) Shortly thereafter, she began seeing Howard Hughes. This pair of lanky publicity-shy lovers caught the fancy of the public and there were almost daily features on their secret meetings and their even more secret plans for the future. Although Hepburn sought to avoid the gossip and speculation, it doubtless drew audiences to the theatre. But despite the play's financial success on the road, *Jane Eyre* was closed in April before it ever reached Broadway. It simply was not strong enough – and Hepburn had learned to fear the critics. She didn't want to return until she had a vehicle in which she felt totally confident.

Meanwhile, RKO had offered her another contract. They needed a good dramatic actress in their stable and after all, she *had* been nominated twice for an Oscar. So the studio gave Hepburn a four-picture deal.

The first picture under the new contract was *Stage Door,* based on a play by Edna Ferber and George S. Kaufman. It was a turning point in Hepburn's career. She played the role of Terry Randall, a stage-struck girl who seems to display little acting talent and less willingness to learn. She had played a similar role in *Morning Glory* only this time she is also a wealthy socialite. She comes to New York and takes up residence at the Footlights Club, where she rooms with a wise-cracking dancer, played by Ginger Rogers. Unbeknownst to Terry, her father agrees to back a play on the condition that she be given the starring role. The producer (Adolphe Menjou at his oiliest) agrees and thus takes the coveted role away from a deserving and talented young dramatic actress (Andrea Leeds) who also lives at the boarding house for Broadway hopefuls. Terry is already unpopular with her fellow residents because of her superior attitude and their hostility deepens when she walks off with the starring role that belonged to another girl. Just before the curtain goes up on opening night, the despondent loser jumps out of a window of the Footlights Club. A badly shaken Terry, who has been abominable in rehearsals, goes on and finds the emotion needed to give a superb performance, gaining the affection of her housemates with a moving curtain speech that pays tribute to the dead girl.

*Stage Door* is bright, lively ensemble playing. Among the residents of the Club are Lucille Ball, Eve Arden and Ann Miller. Franklin Pangborn, Grady Sutton and Jack Carson all have amusing small parts and veteran actress Constance Collier is funny and touching as a superannuated drama coach. The film was directed with a light touch by Gregory LaCava who obtained wonderful performances from all his actors. It was a big hit at the box office and it was also nominated for an Oscar as movie of the year.

Hepburn has two wonderful scenes in *Stage Door.* One is her dramatic curtain speech on opening night. Even better is the scene of her rehearsal for the play, the ''before'' in contrast to the opening night ''after''. She manages to be awkward, wooden, incapable of exhibiting real emotion but all too capable of inappropriate dramatizing. She ignores the director and lectures the playwright on the script's shortcomings. The deadpan way Hepburn utters her opening line, ''The calla lilies are in bloom again,'' struck audiences as being so funny that it became a sort of catchphrase that could break anyone up.

In many ways, the rehearsal scene is similar to the Juliet scene in *Morning Glory* but in the earlier film her ineptitude was presented in a dramatic context. In *Stage Door,* the context is comic which made it more effective. Additional impact came from the fact that Hepburn was willing to exaggerate her own criticized shortcomings to create those of Terry Randall – in fact, as many reviewers noted, the play in *Stage Door* is perilously similar to *The Lake,* Hepburn's most visible failure. It speaks for her maturity as a performer that she was thus able to use her own weaknesses creatively.

*Stage Door* was a success but it was not Hepburn's success alone.

She shared it with the whole ensemble and, in fact, the Oscar nominations went to Andrea Leeds and Gregory LaCava. But the picture was important to her career because it gave RKO the idea that she could be a comedienne which led studio execs to the selection of her next picture: *Bringing Up Baby.*

*Bringing Up Baby* is the quintessential screwball comedy. Hepburn plays the role of Susan Vance, the traditionally madcap heiress. She falls for Professor David Huxley, played with bespectacled confusion by Cary Grant. He is a zoologist devoted to his dinosaur bones, who plans to marry his nice dull secretary. Susan turns his life upside down – he loses a priceless dinosaur bone, alienates the museum's benefactor (Susan's aunt, played by May Robson) and finds himself in unlikely places, such as the middle of a wood searching for a wild leopard and incarcerated in jail. Of course, Susan gets her man and all's right in the end.

It's a brilliant picture. Much of the credit goes to Howard Hawks, who both produced and directed. He obtained a good script by Dudley Nichols and Hagar Wilde and assembled a good supporting cast: Charles Ruggles, Barry Fitzgerald, Fritz Feld, and – not to forget the animal kingdom – Asta, the dog who was such a hit in *The Thin Man* and Nissa, a gorgeous leopard who is the "Baby" of the title.

Hawks, who is best-known for his action pictures, was instrumental in teaching Hepburn how to play comedy. He remembers, "We had a little trouble when starting the picture because Katie rather thought she had to be "funny". She kept laughing, and she took the comic situations too comically. I tried to explain to her that the great clowns – Keaton, Chaplin and Lloyd – simply weren't out there making funny faces; they were serious, sad, solemn and the humour sprang from what happened to them. They'd do funny things in a quiet, sombre deadpan way. Cary understood this at once. Katie didn't."

To help her see what he meant, Hawks brought veteran comic Walter Catlett (under contract to RKO) on the set for a day and asked him to demonstrate a scene, playing Hepburn's part. She got the point at once and in fact, asked Catlett for more help and to insure he'd be around to give it, she got Hawks to offer him a part in the film.

By the time the shooting was over, Hawks spoke highly of Hepburn's talent for comedy. "Once she got the hang of the role, she was wonderful to work with. When she turns, she's in balance, she could knock you out if she wanted to . . . She was a fine tennis player and she had a tennis player's timing in comedy. That marvellous co-ordination!" Critics also appreciated her comic talents. A review in *Life* said, "There has long been a delusion abroad that Miss Hepburn's dramatic talent was confined to a narrow range, and her recent costume pictures seem to prove it. In *Bringing Up Baby*, she leaps into a new and daffy domain already conquered by Carole Lombard and equals Miss Lombard's best." Walter Boehnel commented, "Having proved that she is the cinema's finest dramatic actress, Miss Hepburn now demonstrates that she is a comedienne of the highest order." Even the usually sneering *Time* admitted that Hepburn "proves she can be as amusingly skittery a comedienne as the best of them."

*Bringing Up Baby* is now considered a classic of the genre and many people believe it is Hepburn's best comic performance but at the time of its release, it was not a highly successful movie. It did good business in the major cities but was too highly sophisticated for mass audiences elsewhere. Perhaps it was also badly timed, coming after the interest in screwball comedy had peaked for despite the good reviews, the picture did little to re-establish Hepburn as a box office draw.

Assessing her past record (and no doubt reacting to the notorious "Box Office Poison" ad.) RKO decided that her next picture should be a B comedy called *Mother Carey's Chickens*. Not even Hepburn's self-confidence stretched far enough to make her believe she could rescue that one. She decided to pay RKO $200,000 in lieu of the two pictures she still owed them, and thus, in late 1937, she became a free agent.

It was four months before she found another role. Her good reviews for *Bringing Up Baby*, coupled with her well-known persistence, helped her convince the head of Paramount, Harry Cohn, that she should play the part of Linda Seton in Philip Barry's drawing-room comedy, *Holiday*. Hepburn had understudied the role on Broadway a decade earlier and she knew it was right for her. So was the team already assembled by Paramount: George Cukor as director and Cary Grant as leading man.

*Holiday* is a story that both glamourizes and criticizes the very rich, and then leaves us with a preposterous ending in which the hero virtuously gives up a successful job and marriage to an heiress to "find himself" – on board a luxury liner with another heiress as they go off for a holiday. Cary Grant plays this self-sacrificing (?) Johnny Case, an up-and-coming young man from a working-class background. At the beginning of the picture, he meets and falls in love with Julia Seton (Doris Nolan) on a winter vacation at Lake Placid. Back in New York, he is startled to discover that her family is enormously rich. He tells her, and her stuffy father (Henry Kolker), that as soon as he concludes the big deal he is working on, he intends to go away for as long as it takes to learn who he really is. But neither of them takes this unusual plan seriously. Enter Julia's sister Linda, who thinks Johnny's idea is wonderful and can't understand why her sister disapproves. Linda's efforts to reconcile the lovers have the easily foresee-able effect of causing Linda and Johnny to fall in love. Julia finally breaks the engagement, and the way is clear for Johnny and Linda to board that liner and go off into the sunset.

The role of Linda Seton gives an actress a lot to sink her teeth into. She is intelligent and idealistic but still warmly responsive and fun-loving. She is also a little spoiled, given to some self-dramatizing and capable of real bitchiness. The complexity of the role is challenging and so is the Barry dialogue. Cukor commented insightfully, "His dialogue seemed to be realistic but it wasn't really. The words always had a kind of rhythm underneath them, and the speech was sometimes quite elaborate. He required a particular kind of acting, lightly stylized but not affected." Hepburn was peculiarly suited to such a demand. She was herself a person who only rarely appeared realistic – there was always some degree of stylization about her self-presentation. She even spoke with the same kind of underlying rhythm (she was sometimes criticized for her singsong delivery) and was the ideal Barry heroine.

*Holiday* – with Cary Grant, Edward Everett Horton and Jean Dixon.

40

*The Philadelphia Story* – Hepburn as Tracy Lord with Cary Grant and James Stewart.

*Holiday* gives off a bright shine. The screenplay (an adaptation by Donald Ogden Stewart) is literate and witty. The supporting cast is excellent: Edward Everett Horton as a friend of Johnny's, a professor who comes out of his ivory tower every now and then to drop remarks that cut right through the pretensions around him; Jean Dixon as his loyal wife; Lew Ayres as the dipsomaniac son of the Seton family who shares Linda's ideals but lacks her courage to rebel; Binnie Barnes as an obnoxiously snobby cousin and Doris Nolan as an attractive but ultimately shallow Julia. Cary Grant has the best part in the movie as the self-made man bent on his unmaking (*and* he gets to do a back flip in the last minute of the movie!)

The reviews were good. Howard Barnes said of Hepburn, "As a poor little rich girl, she sustains a dramatic suspense and emotional intensity which the narrative desperately needs. I call this first-class screen acting." Rose Pelswick called her "convincingly wistful." All agreed that George Cukor was a director who knew how to get the best from her. Unfortunately, audiences didn't like *Holiday* as well as the critics did and Hepburn was still unable to dispel the notion that she was not a draw.

*Holiday* was finished in the spring of 1938 and Hepburn went home to Connecticut for a summer of relaxation. She was waiting – and hoping – for the role that would turn her career around. She got it – but it wasn't the one she thought.

Like nearly every other actress under the age of eighty, Hepburn wanted to play Scarlett O'Hara. Producer David Selznick had bought the rights to *Gone With The Wind* and he had hired George Cukor to direct. Hepburn refused to test for the part – she reasoned that both men were familiar with her work and her abilities – but she was sure she was right for it. Selznick seems to have considered her a serious candidate and according to some reports, actually told her she would be his Scarlett. But he later changed his mind. When Hepburn asked why she didn't get the role, he answered, "I just can't imagine Rhett Butler chasing you for ten years." "Well, David," she shot back, "some people's idea of sex appeal is different from yours."

But while Hepburn was vainly chasing the role of Scarlett, something else turned up right under her nose. She had become friendly with Philip Barry and he visited her at her cottage on the Connecticut shore in the fall of 1938. He told her about a new play, written around a heroine he was obviously creating with Hepburn in mind. She listened and became enthusiastic, and *The Philadelphia Story* began to take shape.

Hepburn remembers how it happened. "I got Phil to say he would let the Theatre Guild produce the play . . . *I* didn't know the Guild was in money trouble. *They* didn't know I was finished in Hollywood. *Phil* didn't know about anything, and *I* didn't know that Phil had no idea for the third act. It all just worked. It also made me a star again." Hepburn was totally involved. Because no-one wanted to back the play, she put up one-quarter of the money herself and got Howard Hughes to put up an equal share (the Guild and Barry were the other two investors). She agreed to forego a salary, in return for a percentage of the box office and she busied herself with helping to find the right supporting cast; she was the one who recommended Van Heflin with whom she had worked in *A*  41

*Woman Rebels,* and Joseph Cotton.

   *The Philadelphia Story* opened in New Haven in early 1939. It went onto Philadelphia and Washington whilst Barry tried to find solutions to the problem of the weak third act. There was much debate among the investors about whether the play was strong enough for Broadway but they finally took the gamble and it opened at the Shubert Theatre on March 28. Hepburn tried to conquer her stage fright by mumbling to herself, ''This is Indianapolis, this is Indianapolis.''

   The play was a great hit. The critics were unanimous in their praise of Hepburn who at last felt she was able to put her earlier failure in *The Lake* behind her. *The Philadelphia Story* stayed on Broadway until June, 1940. There was immediate interest in a film version – to which Hepburn had fore-sightedly acquired the rights. She put together a package (herself in the lead, of course, and Cukor to direct) and sold it to Louis B. Mayer at MGM for $250,000. The studio, with Hepburn's approval added Cary Grant and James Stewart as the male leads. Donald Ogden Stewart was again asked to adapt Barry's work for the screen and Joseph L. Mankiewiez was selected to produce.

   The movie was shot in just eight weeks in the summer of 1940. It was a tight deadline because Hepburn was committed to take the play on the road in September. It was a happy set. Cukor and Hepburn always worked well together and she and Grant were also good friends by this, their fourth picture together. And this time they had the support of all the great MGM experts. Hepburn loved the way Joseph Ruttenberg photographed her long thin neck, about which she was exaggeratedly self-conscious. Cedric Gibbons designed perfect sets, in keeping with the understated luxury of the very rich. Adrian's dresses for Hepburn struck just the right note of cool polished elegance.

   Hepburns plays Tracy Lord, an arrogant, aristrocratic young woman from a Philadelphia Mainline family. She is about to marry a stuffed shirt (John Howard) with the usual degree of upper-class privacy. Then a team of reporters arrives on the scene, dispatched through the connivance of her ex-husband (Cary Grant). She haughtily prepares to send them packing but is subjected to a form of blackmail; if they can't write about her, they'll reveal scandalous facts about her black-sheep father. The rest of the movie is devoted to the way Tracy is changed by meeting a situation beyond her control. Early in the film, she is told, ''You'll never be a first-class human being till you learn to have some regard for human frailty;'' later her father accuses, ''You have everything it takes to make a lovely woman except the one essential – an understanding heart.'' The slightly contrived plot teaches Tracy the lesson she needs. She falls in love with a reporter (James Stewart), gets drunk, goes for a midnight swim in the nude and eventually ends up remarrying her first husband. The point of it all is that she too can slip on a banana peel.

   In many ways, Barry modelled Tracy Lord on the persona of Katharine Hepburn. The haughtiness, the air of icy emotional control, the lack of tolerance for other people's failings – all traits that Hepburn projected in her public image. Just as important are the finally displayed warmth and fire, the ultimate willingness to admit that she was wrong. In fact, it is interesting to note the correlation of the sort of personal publicity Hepburn was getting at the time –

much talk of a ''new'' mellower woman who had learned something about patience and humility from the career difficulties of the preceeding years – with the development of Tracy Lord's character.

Film critics loved *The Philadelphia Story*, and it remains a classic. Hepburn was once again nominated for an Oscar, although she lost to Ginger Rogers in *Kitty Foyle*. And at last she had the big box office success to prove herself popular. The national tour of the play in the fall of 1940 became a personal triumph. So conscious was she of what *The Philadelphia Story* had done for her that at the last performance, she emotionally told the audience, ''The curtain will never be rung down on this play'' and walked off the brightly lit stage.

*Bringing Up Baby* – with Gary Grant and Nissa the leopard as 'baby'.

"All right! Yesterday I wasn't anxious enough to be with you."

*Woman Of The Year* – her first picture with Spencer Tracy.

# 5

## Enter Spencer Tracy

*Hepburn wanted to follow up The Philadelphia Story* with another big hit. She found it in a script written by Ring Lardner, Jr. and Michael Kanin (Garson's brother) called *Woman Of The Year*. It was the story of a most unlikely romance between Tess Harding, a hyperkinetic political columnist and Sam Craig, a touch sportswriter for the same newspaper. They fall in love and marry but things do not go well for them. Tess is much too busy and intent upon her career to be the wife Sam wants. Eventually he's had enough and leaves – the very same night she receives an award as Woman Of The Year.

Hepburn took the script to MGM and made another package deal, carefully reserving the right to approve the choice of director and leading man. She asked for and got George Stevens to direct. Her preference for a leading man was Spencer Tracy. She hadn't ever met him in person, but she had seen a number of his movies, and she felt he had the strength to make Sam Craig the natural lord and master of the egotistical Tess. She was disappointed to learn that he was already in Florida preparing to shoot *The Yearling*. But before a second choice could be agreed upon, there was trouble on location, and Tracy returned to Hollywood able and willing to step into a new project.

*Woman Of The Year* was the first of nine Tracy-Hepburn movies and it set the pattern for the workings of this successful team. Tess was a typical Hepburn heroine: bright, verbal, achieving, keeping herself and her life under tight control. As in *The Philadelphia Story,* the plot centres on making the heroine recognize (and suffer for) her human failings. But where Tracy Lord was able to use her intelligence to understand her problem and change her own behaviour by herself, Tess must be forced to it by Sam. This difference is critical.

45

A number of critics have recently commented on the sexism implicit in the plot of *Woman Of The Year* (and other Tracy-Hepburn vehicles as well.) It was just as obvious when the movie was released, of course, but at that time it was generally thought to be one of the film's virtues: "For once, strident Katharine Hepburn is properly subdued," crowed one reviewer. Hepburn herself is perfectly aware of the fact that these movies present an ideal of a dominant male and submissive female. She commented, "I think we represent the perfect American couple. Certainly the ideal American man is Spencer. Sports-loving, a man's man. Strong looking, a big sort of head, boar neck, and so forth. A man. And I think I represent a woman. I needle him and I irritate him, and I try to get around him, yet if he put a big paw out, he could squash me. I think this is the sort of romantic, ideal picture of the male and female in the United States. I'm always sort of skitting about, and he's the big bear, and every once in a while he turns and growls and I tremble. And every once in a while he turns and says some terrible thing and everybody laughs at me, and I get furious. It's very male-female . . ."

The lesson of male dominance is emphasized in the ending of *Woman Of The Year*, although it came about somewhat by accident. Lardner and Kanin had written an ambiguous ending that showed the couple attempting a reconciliation, the success of which was left up in the air. But MGM's Louis B. Mayer insisted that it must have a happy ending. To him, that apparently meant that Tess must overnight be turned into a subservient handmaiden, cheerfully fixing Sam breakfast in bed. The writers were horrified. Producer Joe

*Dragon Seed*

Mankiewicz finally came up with a compromise acceptable to all parties: Tess would march out to the kitchen willing to do her wifely duty at last, but she would prove to be woefully incompetent. The scene is funny but it's not in character. As Gary Carey has pointed out, "It's hard to imagine a woman of her intelligence making the mistake of believing that the way to a man's heart is through the breakfast tray. And even if she did, it seems unlikely that she would be unable to master the use of electric appliances or the art of making a decent waffle."

The chemistry between Tracy and Hepburn that worked so well on the screen also precipitated a romance in real life; it seems that Hepburn herself was among the Americans who found such a male-female relationship ideal. The story of their first meeting on the set is much told. Hepburn, who in those days often wore platform heels and piled her hair on top of her head to make herself look taller and more formidable, looked at medium-height Spencer Tracy and said, "I'm afraid I'm rather tall for you, Mr. Tracy." Producer Mankiewiez, standing nearby, shot back, "Don't worry, he'll cut you down to size." Mankiewiez also recalls the somewhat detrimental effect of their immediate admiration for one another's talent. In the first few days of shooting, he noticed that Hepburn was saying many of her lines in a soft mumble, whereas Tracy was projecting his in a polished and theatrical way. "My God," Mankiewicz exclaimed, "they're imitating each other."

A sense of challenge seemed to pervade their relationship both on and off screen. Hepburn reminisced to Barbara Walters about the first time she

*Without Love* – not one of the better Tracy/Hepburn collaborations.

worked with Tracy. "We had a scene in a restaurant where I reached forward, and I knocked over a glass of water by mistake; I was that excited playing with him, because I admired him so much. And he looked at the glass of water that was turned over and took out his handkerchief and handed it to me. So I thought, the old-son-of-a-bitch, he's not going to get away with that. So I began to mop up. And then I got down under the table and I continued mopping and playing the scene."

In the course of the picture, this challenge turned to warmer feelings. Mankiewicz recalls, "One knew towards the end of the film that they were cosy with each other, and when they had to come back and shoot a new ending, it was quite obvious they were in love." It was a relationship that continued until Tracy's death in 1967 but it was carried on with astonishing discretion. Almost nothing appeared in print until well into the 1960s; if they were ever mentioned as being in the same place at the same time, it was always with a list of other people and they were tactfully referred to as "friends". What made the gossip-hungry press behave with such protectiveness? No doubt many journalists were thrown off the scent by the great circumspection of the lovers. Their visits to one another's sets were completely secret, they never even stayed in the same hotel and the time they spent together was very private and almost never involved going out in public. And perhaps when reporters did catch on, they remained silent because of the obvious sincerity of the couple's preference for privacy.

One of the reasons for such discretion was the fact that Tracy was married and the father of two children. He and his wife had drifted apart before he met Hepburn but as Catholics, they were reluctant to divorce. Moreover, it seems unlikely that Hepburn (always careful to defend Louise Tracy's dignity) wanted to become the second Mrs. Tracy. She had often gone on record saying she thought marriage was not for her – and maybe not for anyone in her profession. "An actor should never marry, not even another actor. You're too involved with yourself, and your work is too demanding, to give the necessary amount of attention to another human being. Inevitably, that person feels left out. And becomes unhappy."

Perhaps it was her willingness to face this limitation that permitted Hepburn to remain so devoted for 25 years. Simone Signoret, who knew her in the 60s, observed that every day at 4.30 Hepburn disappeared, "like a school-girl in love;" she dropped whatever she was doing and went off to shop for and cook Spencer Tracy's dinner. She took care of him as his health declined, and for the last five years of his life, she turned down all work so she could be with him. His death was a hard blow.

Their pleasure in working together never diminished, and surely it is part of the success of so many of the movies they made as a team. *Woman Of The Year* was nearly as big a hit as *The Philadelphia Story*. Although Otis Ferguson complained that the plot "loses ground when the audience perceives that such a fine type of man would never go all the way down the line for such a uselessly preeminent bitch," even he admitted that Hepburn had "never before been able to condense into one performance so much of her almost outrageous challenge and appeal, deliberate affection and genuine, delightful ease." Donald Kirkley

48

said, "Her performance in *Woman Of The Year* shows . . . subtlety and depth . . . her performance is a constant pleasure to watch." *Time* said Hepburn and Tracy succeeded "in turning several batches of cinematic corn into passable moonshine." Hepburn was once again nominated for an Oscar, but the award went to Greer Garson in *Mrs. Miniver*. Only Lardner and Kanin actually won for their screenplay.

Woman Of The Year was finished just a short time before the attack on Pearl Harbour that brought America into World War II. Hepburn's next film project somehow got mixed up with a lot of patriotic intentions. *Keeper Of The Flame*, based on a novel by I.A.R. Wylie, is the story of the efforts of a national hero's widow to keep quiet his shameful secret: that he was in private life a Fascist. Hepburn, of course, would play the gallant widow whose concern for "keeping the flame" is based on her desire not to upset the nation at a time of great peril and Tracy was cast as Steven O'Malley, a reporter who scents the secret. This is the only Tracy-Hepburn picture in which their characters are not romantically involved.

Louis B. Mayer liked the plot idea, apparently failing to recognize that the character of the Fascist was based in large part on his friend William Randolph Hearst. Donald Ogden Stewart, chairman of Hollywood's Anti-Nazi League, was engaged to write the script. While that was in process, Hepburn took time off to tour in a new Philip Barry play, *Without Love*.

Hepburn was hoping to repeat the magic success of *The Philadelphia Story*, but the new play was obviously much weaker. Another problem was the casting of the leading man. Somehow the Theatre Guild had ended up with Elliott Nugent, a competent actor but quite unsuited for his role. Garson Kanin went to see the play in Wilmington, Delaware and spoke to Hepburn after the curtain. She knew the play was in trouble and asked for his advice. He cracked, "You and Nugent should change parts." She found it distinctly unfunny but Kanin's joke was right on target: it was Hepburn who dominated when it should have been Nugent. After a few months on the road, all concerned agreed that the script needed more work so Barry started a heavy rewrite and Hepburn went back to California to shoot *Keeper Of The Flame*.

George Cukor directed the picture and he is candid about its shortcomings. "The original novel was a bit hokey-pokey and pretentious. And we shot *everything* on the sound stage, even the outdoor scenes . . . Everyone looked like a waxwork in Madame Tussaud's. And when an old woman went mad, we had a raging artificial snowstorm with prop room lightning." Cukor was also disappointed with Hepburn's performance and thought she was too stagey an artificial. "It was very much a *Christopher Strong* performance; she was always coming on in something glittering in that one and delivering long theatrical speeches and now she was doing it again." Of course, it's hardly fair to blame Hepburn for the inadequacies of the part. Cukor recalls sympathetically, "In her first scene she had to float in wearing a long white gown and carrying a bunch of lilies (calla lilies as it happens). That's awfully tricky, isn't it?"

Tracy gave a strong performance as the persistent reporter and a number of critics have singled out the contribution of Percy Kilbride (later to be cast as Pa Kettle) in the small comic role of the taxi driver. But the film has more 49 atmosphere than plot, more message than feeling and it degenerates into an absurdly melodramatic ending, in which the widow, in the act of at last confessing her husband's secret, is shot by his still-loyal secretary, who then sets fire to the house.

When the shooting was over, Hepburn returned to *Without Love*, which opened on Broadway on November 1, 1942. Barry had not completely licked the script problems and the play was not the success Hepburn had hoped for. Although most reviewers generously allowed for the weakness of the material, some nevertheless pointed out that her performance was not up to the high standard of *The Philadelphia Story*. *Without Love* ran for 113 performances and during that time, Hepburn managed to squeeze in a cameo appearance in *Stage Door Canteen,* a film that was made to benefit the servicemen's canteens operated by the American Theatre Wing. Like the sixty-five other stars who contributed their services, she played herself. She appears near the end of the picture, consoling a young hostess at a canteen who has just learned that her fiancé's ship has sailed before they could be married.

*Undercurrent* – with Robert Taylor.

One hopes Hepburn's next film was also embarked upon for patriotic reasons. Her old friend Pandro Berman was now a producer at MGM, and he asked her to play the role of Jade in *Dragon Seed*. Based on the novel by Pearl S. Buck, it tells the story of the young Chinese peasant girl who decides to join in the guerilla fighting against the Japanese invaders of her country. MGM presumably saw an opportunity to support the war effort and make money at the same time; after all, the last movie made from a Buck novel about China, *The Good Earth*, had been a box-office hit.

*Dragon Seed* got the full production treatment. At a cost of $2 million, MGM turned several acres of southern California into a Chinese landscape – building terraces, actually *painting* the ground to make it look more contoured and laying miles of water pipes to flood fields and create instant rice paddies. With the scenery complete, the interest in authenticity abruptly vanished. Out of a cast of thirty three, only three actors were Oriental. The makeup department did the best they could with Hepburn, Agnes Moorhead, Walter Huston, Akim Tamiroff and Hurd Hatfield but the results were not particularly convincing. The critics couldn't resist a few jabs. James Agee said Hepburn looked "awful and silly" in her "shrewdly tailored Peck and Peckish pyjamas"; the *Cue* reviewer commented that it was "hard to accept Katharine Hepburn's New England twang and sharply Anglo-Saxon features as Chinese." But they all agreed she did as well as could be expected under the circumstances.

Hepburn had already decided what she intended to do next; she wanted to make a film version of *Without Love*. MGM had bought the rights to it, just to be on the safe side, when it first opened in Broadway but Louis B. Mayer had cooled toward the project when it turned out to be less successful than *The Philadelphia Story*. He was persuaded, however, by producer Lawrence Weingarten that it could make a good vehicle for Hepburn and Tracy with Donald Ogden Stewart writing the screenplay minus the heavy political message that had marred the play.

In the stage version, the hero is an Irish-American politician and he makes several long speeches about the reasons that Ireland ought to enter the war. Stewart's screenplay changed the politician to a scientist and emphasized the farcical elements of Barry's work. Spencer Tracy plays the now-scientist Pat Jamieson, a man who is having trouble finding a place to live in Washington because of the wartime housing shortage. Katharine Hepburn plays a widow with a big house. Somehow their marriage – on a Platonic basis only – comes to seem a patriotic duty. But of course proximity does its work and they finally admit to one another that they no longer want their marriage to be "without love."

Hepburn had hoped Cukor could direct but he was otherwise engaged so she suggested Harold Bucquet, who had been the director of *Dragon Seed*. Irene made her stylish wardrobe and Lucille Ball and Keenan Wynn were given the comic supporting roles. Hepburn followed her usual custom of trying to be involved in every little detail. Producer Weingarten remembers, "People always said to me, 'She's trying to do everything.' And my reply was, 'The thing I'm afraid of is that she *can* do everything.' Producer, director, cameraman! That's what she was!" Pandro Berman, put the same point in a slightly more irritated way, after he worked with her again on *Dragon Seed*. "Kate was just as big a louse when I worked with her in her struggling days. I don't mean that literally – I was still fond of her. But, God, she was tough! She was difficult – but even when she drove you mad, you had to admire her spunk, her guts. She got exactly what she wanted – wouldn't work any later than she thought she should, wanted triple overtime – but when she was on the set, she toiled like a bridge-mender."

*Without Love* was certainly more successful than the previous Tracy-Hepburn picture, *Keeper Of The Flame*. Of course, it helped that they played a romantic couple again and that they both had a few good lines. Tracy made it believable that for most of the picture he was more interested in his work than in the beautiful woman he lived with and he even accomplished the trickier part of making his eventual capitulation to love seem in character. This change was the essence of Tracy's contribution to the team. For most of each picture, he would seem self-sufficient, tolerant of the stings administered by Hepburn because they didn't penetrate his masculine armour. Then at some point near the end, he reveals his vulnerability (often in a great display of temper) and suddenly we see him as more romantic and more deeply devoted even than Hepburn.

Director Harold Bucquet (who died shortly after the film was completed) commented at the time on the difference in their acting styles that mirrored this difference in their dramatic personae. "Directing Mr. Tracy amounts to telling him when you're ready to start a scene. He hasn't let me down yet, and if he does, perhaps we'll get acquainted. Miss Hepburn requires direction, for she tends to act too much. Her acting is much less economical than Mr. Tracy's, but his style is rubbing off on her."

Although *Without Love* is not one of the strongest Tracy-Hepburn films, it was a reasonable success at the time and the critics were very favourable. Perhaps that explains why MGM again allowed them to choose their next picture.

Both Tracy and Hepburn had read and loved the Conrad Richter novel, *The Sea Of Grass* and Tracy has asked MGM to buy the rights so he could appear as the cattle baron from New Mexico, Colonel James Brewton, a man who is almost mystically attached to the grasslands of his home. Unfortunately, the novel had no female lead; Brewton's wife appears only briefly at the beginning and end of the book. So when Hepburn expressed an interest in the project, screenwriters Marguerite Roberts and Vincent Lawrence had to beef up the wife's part and invent some reason for her long absence. They came up with the idea of an affair with her husband's enemy, a Denver lawyer who won the court decision to open the grasslands to homesteaders. So the pastoral story of a man's brooding love for the land became embellished with some fantastic soap opera twists: an illegitimate son fathered by the lawyer but accepted by Brewton; the son's death in a duel and a last-minute reconciliation of the Brewtons. The film was probably doomed from the start by this split-personality script.

Things got even worse when producer Pandro Berman selected Elia Kazan to direct. One guesses that he was chosen because of his recent
52   success with the realistic drama *A Tree Grows In Brooklyn*, but Kazan soon

discovered that MGM intended to let no such realism creep into *The Sea Of Grass.* He wanted to shoot on location; they insisted that the actors simply stand in front of back-projected footage of the Nebraska plains. He wanted simple home-spun costumes; Walter Plunkett was told to create more than 30 elaborate dresses for Hepburn. (Someone on the set commented, "It was one of those pictures in which every time Kate went to the bathroom, she came back in a new costume.") And it soon became obvious that Kazan was not the right director for Tracy. Kazan emphasized a psychological approach, digging into the motivation and feelings of the characer; Tracy was an intuitive actor who once claimed the secret of his art was "Learn your lines and don't bump into the furniture."

The picture was not a success. Bosley Crowther said, "Miss Hepburn's performance as Tracy's helpmate is so rigidly attitudinized that her scenes, either alone or with others, are distressingly pompous and false." Others commented that it was hard to tell the difference between Tracy's mystic communion with the grasslands and an acute attack of boredom.

Before *The Sea Of Grass* was released, Hepburn made another picture, *Undercurrent* – alas, no more successful. She played the part of Ann Hamilton, first glimpsed as a sort of dreamy-eyed bobbysoxer, the daughter of a college professor Edmund Gwenn, (who had also played Hepburn's father in *Sylvia Scarlett*). She is swept off her feet by a rich industrialist (is there ever a poor one in the movies?) played by Robert Taylor. After she marries him, she begins to notice his strange attitude toward his brother (Robert Mitchum) who may or may not be dead. The film is meant to have the haunting quality of *Rebecca* or *Suspicion* but the script was simply too weak and the final unmasking of the husband as a vicious killer comes as little surprise. Director Vincente Minelli did his best and he had a talented cast to work with but *Undercurrent* went down because of the limitations of its melodramatic script.

With *Undercurrent* and then *The Sea Of Grass* flopping at the box office, MGM further damaged Hepburn's career by casting her in *Song Of Love,* a soppy biography of Robert Schumann and his wife Clara. Paul Henreid played Schumann, a struggling young composer who meets and marries the brilliant pianist Clara Wieck. She gives up her career and devotes herself to caring for her husband, who is unappreciated by the public, and her seven children. Somewhere along the way, the Schumanns take in as a boarder/student young Johannes Brahms (played by Robert Walker, who had the part of Hepburn's son in *The Sea Of Grass*). He falls in love with Clara but she refuses to leave her husband. Eventually, Schumann breaks down in despair over his lack of recognition and then dies in an asylum. Clara returns to the keyboard and (under a gigantic bust of her dear departed hsuband) gives a concert that brings his music to an appreciative audience at last.

Hepburn threw herself into *Song Of Love* with her customary vigour, insisting on taking months of lessons to learn to finger the keyboard correctly so the concert scenes would be convincing. But even *her* energy, the beautiful costumes by Walter Plunkett and Irene and the recorded piano music by Artur Rubinstein were not enough to save this picture.

Hepburn's next picture didn't come until the summer of 1948 – and it was an accident that she was in it at all. Howard Lindsay and Russell 53

Crouse wrote a play in 1945 called *State Of The Union,* about an aspiring politician who forgets that the end doesn't justify the means. Hepburn was offered the part of the politician's wife (who is also his conscience) but turned it down. The play was a hit; it ran two years and won a Pulitzer Prize. Frank Capra bought the movie rights and brought it to MGM, where studio execs wanted it as a vehicle for Gary Cooper and Claudette Colbert. Cooper was unavailable, but Colbert agreed, and Tracy was finally selected to play the politician. The week before shooting was to begin, Colbert dropped out. Tracy suggested to Capra that Hepburn, who had been helping him learn his lines, might come to the rescue. Capra remembers gratefully, "On the phone, Hepburn wasted no words on contracts or salary or billing. A show was in distress. She was being asked to help. And help she did."

In *State Of The Union,* Hepburn plays the part of the estranged wife of Grant Mathews, a businessman who has decided to make a run for the Presidency. In order to help his candidacy, she tours with her husband and appears at his side. But her advice to maintain his integrity is outweighed by the machinations of his present girl-friend, a powerful newspaper publisher (Angela Lansbury) and the old-line politician who is managing his campaign (Adolphe Menjou). Grant Mathews is finally stung into an awareness of the corruption and deceit into which he is sinking when he sees his wife gallantly attempt for his sake to make a radio speech that she knows to be a pack of lies. Husband and wife are reconciled and Mathews decides to drop out of the race in order to speak his mind freely to the people.

It's the kind of movie – a mix of soap opera, idealism, and comedy – that Frank Capra does perfectly, and even though *State Of The Union* is not his best film, it still holds up well. Lansbury is striking as the treacherous other woman, and Van Johnson has a very effective part as a wise-cracking reporter whose cynicism is only a mask for his idealistic principles. There's a wonderful small part for Maidel Truner as a Southern judge's wife who consumes glass after glass of a cocktail called a Sazerac without ever bothering to inquire what it contains and Margaret Hamilton is also good in a small part as a housekeeper with a crush on the reporter.

*State Of The Union* got a mixed reception. Some critics were impressed whilst others decried the whole affair. *Time* was particularly harsh: the review characterized Tracy as lacking fire and said, "Hepburn's affectation of talking like a woman simultaneously trying to steady a loose dental brace sharply limits her range of expression." But Howard Barnes said Hepburn was "restrained and persuasive and altogether delightful" and the Times called her charming. A prominent fan of the picture was President Truman despite the fact that he was the butt of several of the best jokes.

If *State Of The Union* helped to get Tracy and Hepburn back on the track, their next picture, *Adam's Rib,* won the race. The screenplay was written for them by their friends Garson Kanin and Ruth Gordon. It was produced by Lawrence Weingarten, who had also become a friend and it was directed by George Cukor, another close friend. Walter Plunkett turned out Hepburn's wardrobe, and another friend, Cole Porter, even volunteered to write a song for the film (that caused the heroine's name to be changed to Amanda, because

54

From Illustrated, March 22nd, 1947.

55

Porter refused to write a song about anyone named Madeline.)

Tracy and Hepburn play a pair of married lawyers. Adam Bonner, who works in the District Attorney's office, is given the job of prosecuting a dizzy blonde housewife (Judy Holliday) who followed her husband to his girlfriend's house and shot him. Amanda Bonner, in private practice, is incensed over the double standard that countenances male infidelity and supports the notion of female inequality, so she jumps in to defend the wife. It doesn't take long for the fight in the courtroom to spill over into the Bonners' home life and, when the trial ends, it seems that their marriage will too. But Amanda admits she has gone too far and there is a happy ending.

*Adam's Rib* was the felicitous result of the collaboration of talented people who knew each other well. Hepburn has commented that the Kanins know how to write for the Tracy-Hepburn team. "Married couples can see themselves in us . . . Competing and yet not competing . . . The woman very quick, on to everything, ready to go forward with anything, emotional. The man slower, more solid, very funny at times, good with quips, ultimately subduing the woman, thereby making her happy because she really wanted to be subdued, or at least to let him think she's being subdued." And Cukor as director knew how to capitalize on that relationship. The result is a bright, quick, quippy film that leaves a bad aftertaste. Tracy's dominance at the end of the movie is established with such a heavy hand and such unfair tactics that it seems meanspirited.

Today's viewer might find *Adam's Rib* most successful when it turns away from the Bonners' power struggles. Judy Holliday is excellent as the would-be murderess (Hepburn had fought to get her the part); the on-location photography in New York adds welcome realism; Cukor and the Kanins managed to capture all the authentic little details, like small talk at a party, or the look of a professional couple's apartment. When the movie was released, the critics were all enthusiastic and it was a big success at the box office in the winter

*Song Of Love* – with Leo G. Carroll (left) and Paul Henreid.

of 1949-1950. Both Tracy and Hepburn suddenly found that they were offered challenging roles on their own with the result that only three more Tracy-Hepburn films were made.

The next was *Pat And Mike,* made in 1952 as the last film under Hepburn's contract to MGM. It reunited the same team that made *Adam's Rib* with even more successful results. The idea for the film came from Garson Kanin, as he watched Hepburn destroy an opponent on the tennis court; he commented to his wife that Hepburn ought to do a picture that would use her considerable athletic talents to real advantage. So they whipped up a script about a lady athlete, Pat Pemberton, who signs a contract for professional management with a tough-talking sports promoter, Mike Conovan (Tracy's role). Her only weakness is that she can't perform when her fiancé (William Ching) is watching and this leads to an involved plot with some Runyonesque gangsters trying to manipulate the results of a golf tournament.

*Pat And Mike* is a light amusing movie and this time the struggle between Tracy and Hepburn for the upper hand seems less objectionable — perhaps because it begins in the context of a professional relationship rather than a personal one. Their romance is underplayed, submerged in the athlete/manager relationship, a fact which is emphasized by comparison with the manager's relationship with another athlete in his stable (Aldo Ray playing a dumb boxer.)

With its fast-moving scenes using real-life professional athletes, its comic gangsters and some good performances from minor characters such as Sunny White, Chuck Connors, and Charles Bronson, *Pat And Mike* was a hit with the mass audiences. Critics liked it too. Bosley Crowther said Hepburn showed "she can swing a golf club or tennis racquet as adroitly as she can swing an epigram," and *Time* called the film one of the season's gayest comedies.

The next Tracy-Hepburn movie was not made until 1957. (They are always called Tracy-Hepburn movies because Tracy always insisted on top billing. When Garson Kanin once suggested that sometimes ladies ought to be allowed to go first, Tracy replied, "This is a movie, not a lifeboat.") The husband-and-wife writing team of Henry and Phoebe Ephron decided to do a screen adaptation of William Marchant's hit play *Desk Set*. They approached Hepburn for the lead role (played by Shirley Booth on stage) and she was interested. She also proposed that the part of the computer inventor be built up for Tracy; he had just finished the gruelling job of shooting *The Old Man And The Sea,* and she thought he would welcome a chance to do light comedy. So the script was rewritten, and Twentieth-Century-Fox agreed to make the picture.

Hepburn plays Bunny Watson, a reference librarian with a mind like a steel trap, who thinks she's in love with one of the company executives (Gig Young). She and her staff (among them Joan Blondell and Dina Merrill) are alarmed to discover that a computer is going to be installed in their department — they assume it means they will lose their jobs. But all is well in the end. No one is fired and Bunny discovers the man she really loves is the computer inventor.

The plot of *Desk Set* is not particularly convincing, but there's some good sharp dialogue, notably in the sparring between Hepburn and Tracy when they first meet. And they have a long funny scene that starts with a ride    57

58

*Adam's Rib.*

home from the office, continues through barbed seduction during the fixing of dinner, and ends with the sudden appearance of the other man: the whole thing is a treasure. The film's lightness of touch may have caused some people to underrate it but the critics were favourable even if a trifle condescending.

Hepburn didn't make another film with Tracy for ten years. In 1967, Stanley Kramer, with whom Tracy has previously worked on several films, approached him with the idea of a comedy that also addressed the social issue of integration. William Rose would write the screenplay and Kramer thought he could get Sidney Poitier for the role of the black doctor with whom the daughter of a liberal white couple falls in love. Kramer knew that Tracy was ill and frail but he thought there was no one else who could carry the part. After some debate, Tracy agreed to do the picture and Hepburn took the part of his wife; Poitier signed on and Hepburn got Kramer to agree to cast her niece, Katharine Houghton, in the role of the daughter. One obstacle came when Columbia tried to take out the usual insurance against the losses caused by an unfinished picture; the state of Tracy's health was so bad no one would insure the picture. Kramer and Hepburn solved the problem by putting up their salaries in lieu of the insurance.

Kramer called *Guess Who's Coming To Dinner* a "social comedy" and emphasized its meassage but many critics were quick to point that the script loaded the situation so much in the black doctor's favour that it undercut the issue; as someone commented, the man had all the qualifications for sainthood. But Tracy and Hepburn rose above the limitations of the material to give moving performances. Unquestionably, part of the effectiveness of the film was due to Kramer's willingness to lean on what the audience knows of the real lives of the actors. This happens most poignantly near the end of the film when the father delivers a speech telling the young couple that he remembers what it is to have loved; the machinery of the plot drops away and we are looking at Spencer Tracy and Katharine Hepburn in a private moment. Even all these years later, that scene is still painful to watch.

Critics may have been divided over the question of whether *Guess Who's Coming To Dinner* really made any significant social point but all agreed that the performances were first-rate. In addition to the four principals, Cecil Kellaway had some good moments as a cleric who is called in as a friend of the family; Roy E. Glenn, Sr. and Beah Richards made the most of their appearance as the doctor's parents and Isabell Sanford was brilliant as the white couple's maid who disapproves of the match.

Two and a half weeks after the shooting of the picture was finished, Spencer Tracy died. Hepburn faced the loss bravely and, after a period of seclusion, threw herself into her work. When Oscar nominations were announced at the end of the year, both Hepburn and Tracy were on the list. By the time of the Awards ceremony, she was on location in France, so she got the news when a housekeeper telephoned her from Hollywood. She had won her third Oscar.

"Did Mr. Tracy win it too?" she asked.

"No, Ma'am."

"Well, that's okay, I'm sure mine is for the two of us."

*Summertime* with Rossano Brazzi.

# 6

## The Great Dramatic Parts

*Katharine Hepburn took a risk* few actresses would dare when she agreed to star in *The African Queen*. She played a bony self-righteous old maid, a woman with a plain exterior and a prickly personality. In her early forties – an age many leading ladies find awkward, if not downright threatening – she was made up to appear fifty-five, and the camera showed every wrinkle, vein and freckle in Technicolor (it was Hepburn's first colour film.) The result of this gamble was rave reviews, increased respect for her dramatic talent and an Oscar nomination.

The rights to the C. S. Forester novel had been purchased by director John Huston and producer Sam Spiegel. Humphrey Bogart was their one and only choice for the role of Charlie Allnut, the hard-drinking riverboat captain. Bogart and Huston then agreed that the role of Rose Sayer, the spinster missionary who forces Charlie to become both a hero and a lover, should be offered to Hepburn.

It was 1951, and she had finished *Adam's Rib* and gone on to play Rosalind in a Broadway production of *As You Like It*. She agreed immediately and obtained permission from MGM, to whom she still owed one more picture. In April, the cast went on location in Africa, in what was then the Belgian Congo. It was the first time Hepburn had shot a movie outside Hollywood and it was a tough experience. There were crocodiles in the river, poisonous snakes in the portable toilet and germs in the water. The set was attacked by soldier ants; Hepburn got skin cancer from being out all day in the fierce equatorial sun; everyone was ill from the food and water – Hepburn worst of all because she had primly refused to join the others in drinking Jack Daniels bourbon as a substitute

61

for water.

Despite all the problems, she threw herself into the experience enthusiastically. Bogart later spoke of his first impression. "She talked a blue streak. We listened for the first couple of days and then began asking ourselves, 'How affected can you be in the middle of Africa?' She used to say that everything was 'divine.' 'Oh, what a divine native!' she'd say. 'Oh, what a divine pile of manure!' You had to ask yourself, 'Is this realy the dame or is this something left over from *Woman Of The Year*?'" But their respect for one another's craft soon made Hepburn and Bogart friends and it also made them a strong team on the scren.

*The African Queen* is an adventure story, a chase movie, a drama, a comedy and a romance all rolled into one. It begins with the meeting of Rose and Charlie in 1914 at her brother's African mission, when Rose tries to serve tea as if she were in a country house in Surrey and Charlie talks on and on about the noises his stomach makes. When Rose's brother (Robert Morley) dies, Charlie offers her refuge from the oncoming German soldiers on his dilapidated boat. Once aboard, Rose insists that they make a perilous trek downriver to attack a German gunboat and thus pave the way for the landing by British troops. During the long trip, Rose gradually reveals her feminine vulnerability, while Charlie learns to treat her protectively; by the time they reach their objective, they are in love. Before they can complete their plans to attack the German ship, a storm comes up and the pair are removed from the swamped *African Queen* by the German crew. They are to be hanged as spies but Charlie asks that they be married first. Their lives are saved at the crucial moment because the German ship runs into their little boat of explosives. They find themselves blown overboard, swimming for freedom.

The screenplay was written by James Agee, working closely with Huston. There are some wonderful lines; among the best, Hepburn's comment that, "Nature is what we are put into the world to rise above." Huston has said that neither he nor Agee realized as they were writing the extent of the comedy implicit in the film. It emerged of its own accord as Bogart and Hepburn began playing off one another and it's what makes *The African Queen* so effective. Each shows a relish of the other's absurdity that makes this improbable romance believable – at least for the duration of the picture. A bit of shrewd direction from Huston helped to make the lovers' relationship even better. He had observed that Hepburn, in trying to emphasize the gap between Rose and Charlie, was treating him like a servant. He suggested instead that she behave like a great lady trying to do her best under unfortunate circumstances. The lady he mentioned as a model was Eleanor Roosevelt. "Smile, pour out the gin, smile. Whatever you do, smile."

Many people rate this Hepburn's best performance and the critics, then and now, have been admiring. Pauline Kael calls *The African Queen* "one of the most charming and entertaining movies ever made;" Bosley Crowther said Hepburn was "fluttery and airy in her very best comedy style;" *Cue* said the performances were "unmatched by anything Hepburn and Bogart have yet contributed to the screen." The movie grossed over $4 million in the US alone, a very successful film in its day. Hepburn, Bogart, Huston and Agee and

With Bogart in *The African Queen*. Often rated as her best screen performance.

Huston for the screenplay were all nominated for Academy Awards. Only Bogart won (Vivien Leigh was named Best Actress for her work in *Streetcar Named Desire*) but he credited Hepburn with enabling him to give the performance.

When shooting on *The African Queen* was over, Hepburn returned to Hollywood to make *Pat And Mike* with Spencer Tracy. It was the last film of her MGM contract and she never signed another. She celebrated her freedom by throwing herself into a play, this time on the London stage. She had decided she wanted to play Epifania, the leading character of George Bernard Shaw's play *The Millionairess*. She toured the provinces in the spring of 1952 and opened in June at the New Theatre. Although most critics agree that Shaw's play is weak and wordy, Hepburn herself received very generous notices. *The Millionairess* closed in London in September and opened in New York a month later for a limited ten-week run. American critics and audiences were not quite so kind as the English and the production barely cleared its costs.

But Hepburn was not through with Epifania. She believed it was a part that suited her, or at least that expressed aspects of the worst side of her character. Epifania is domineering, arrogant, a monster of egotism; as someone put it, she is what Tracy Lord might have grown up to be if she hadn't learned to confront her humanity. Hepburn wanted to play the part on the screen so she bought the film rights, worked with Preston Sturges to produce a screenplay and finally tried to sell the whole package, just as she'd done so successfully with *The Philadelphia Story*. But she found no takers and by the spring of 1953, she regretfully shelved the project.

She found instead another screen adaptation of a play. David Lean had bought the rights to *The Time Of The Cuckoo,* which had been a hit on Broadway with Shirley Booth in the lead role. It was the story of a middle-aged American spinster who goes to Venice for a vacation and falls in love with an Italian shopkeeper – who, she finds out, is married and the father of a family. The play suggests that the spinster is a lonely misfit who tries to delude herself into believing she is the heroine of a great romance. When Lean wrote the screenplay (in collaboration with H.E. Bates) he softened the story to make the spinster more sympathetic and the love story more genuine. *Summertime,* as the screen version was called in America (it was titled *Summer Madness* in England) seems in tone very like an earlier Lean film, *Brief Encounter*. Interspersed with the bittersweet romance are comic scenes of the American abroad but although they make her vulnerable, they never go so far as to make her ridiculous.

Hepburn quickly agreed to play the role of Jane Hudson, and Rossano Brazzi was cast as the Italian with whom she falls in love. The film was shot on location in Venice in the summer of 1954, and Lean used the golden Italian cityscape almost as another character in the drama – a force instrumental in changing, softening and releasing Jane.

Working on location proved to have one serious drawback. In one scene, Hepburn was to become so engrossed in photographing the splendors of Venice that she falls into the canal – and it only worked if she did the stunt herself. She remembers, ''I knew how dirty the water was, so I took all kinds of precautions – even washed my mouth with antiseptic, put special dressing on my hair, wore shoes that wouldn't waterlog. but like an idiot, I forgot my eyes . . .

*The Lion In Winter* with Peter O'Toole.

*The Iron Petticoat* – Hope and Hepburn's unsuccessful attempt at recycling Garbo's *Ninotchka*.

*The Rainmaker* with Lloyd Bridges (seated right).

*On Golden Pond* with Henry Fonda.

*The Corn Is Green.*

Well, the water was a *sewer!* Filthy – brackish – full of trash. When I got out, my eyes were running. They've been running ever since. I have the most ghastly infection – I'll never lose it 'til the day I die.''

The reviews of *Summertime* were excellent. *Time* said, ''Few actresses in films could equal Hepburn's evocation of aching loneliness on her first night in Venice as she wanders, forlorn and proud, like a primly starched ghost in a city of lovers.'' Rose Pelswick said she made the most of her ''characterization as the shy and lonely dreamer.'' The *New Yorker* called her ''wonderfully effective, making the most of her opportunities for registering pathos and passion and turning in a couple of first-rate slapstick sequences as well.'' She received another Academy Award nomination, her sixth, although the winner turned out to be Anna Magnani for *The Rose Tattoo.*

In the spring of 1955, Hepburn returned to the stage in a tour of Australia with the Old Vic Company. She appeared as Kate in *Taming Of The Shrew*, Portia in *The Merchant Of Venice,* and Isobella in *Measure For Measure.* Although critics were caustic about her voice and accent, and compared her unfavourably with Vivien Leigh who had toured there several years earlier, the performances were generally sold out and Hepburn herself greatly enjoyed the trip.

Her next film, made in London, is generally considered to be one of her worst. She was shown a script by writer Ben Hecht for a film called *The Iron Petticoat* that recycles the plot of Garbo's *Ninotchka.* Captain Vinka Kovelenko, in a fit of petulant anger, defects to an American air base in West Germany. An American pilot is assigned to convert her to capitalism and, after some sparring, she yields to the lure of Western luxuries and true love. Ralph Thomas signed on to direct and then someone got the bright idea to cast Bob Hope as the GI persuader. It might have worked, under a very strong directorial hand that pushed Hope into playing more subtly, in the style of romantic comedy. But he was allowed to perform as a gagman which immediately destroyed any illusion the rest of the film might have managed to create. He also called in his own writers to punch up his lines and so much of the original script disappeared that Hecht withdrew his name and later publicly apologized to Hepburn for landing her in such a mess. As Hope's part grew, Hepburn's shrank, and much of her sole comic footage was edited out. None of her scenes with Hope is a success: their styles of comedy simply cancel one another out. Bosley Crowther said Hepburn's ''Russian affectation and accent are simply horrible,'' and William K. Zinsser cracked, ''Where Miss Hepburn, encased in an army uniform that does nothing for her lissome figure, turns to Bob Hope and says, 'I vas vorried,' she has good reason.''

While the editors were still hacking up *The Iron Petticoat,* Hepburn went along with Spencer Tracy to location in Cuba for *The Old Man And The Sea.* When he went back to film the studio scenes in Hollywood, she began her next film, *The Rainmaker.* It was another adaptation of a play, to which Paramount held the screen rights. Producer Hal Wallis signed the original Broadway director, Joseph Anthony and then cast Katharine Hepburn and Burt Lancaster in the lead roles.

70         In *The Rainmaker,* Hepburn plays another frustrated spinster. This

*Desk Set* – with Joan Blondell.

*Suddenly, Last Summer* – with Montgomery Clift and Elizabeth Taylor.
The screenplay by Gore Vidalwas based on the Tennessee Williams' play.

74

With Ralph Richardson in *A Long Day's Journey Into Night*.

time she is a middle-aged woman living on a farm, taking care of her father and two brothers. Along comes a con man (Burt Lancaster) who is trying to convince the drought-ridden town that for a slight fee he can produce rain. but his real success is metaphorical rather than literal, as he succeeds in convincing plain Lizzie Curry that she is capable of blossoming into an attractive feminine woman who is ready to love and be loved. As reviewers were quick to point out, Lizzie is really a country cousin of Jane Hudson.

There are a number of things about *The Rainmaker* that are not quite right. One problem is that it was shot in a studio and therefore conveys little sense of a parched and waiting landscape, the physical parallel of Lizzie's spiritual condition. Another problem is that, as someone pointed out long ago about *Spitfire,* Hepburn is not suited to playing primitives. She is too mannered, too self-conscious, too civilized. She also has the wrong accent for a country girl in the southwest (although one has to admit it is preferable to listen to her natural way of speaking, no matter how unsuitable, than to sit through her various attempts at doing accents.)

A more serious flaw is the lack of spark between Hepburn and Lancaster. Although he is well cast as the fast-talking charlatan and easily believable in his exchanges with all other characters, there is no real sense of attraction when he and Hepburn are on the screen together. There are rumours that they did not get on well personally; he found her much too affected and she didn't care for his Hollywood approach to acting (for example, he learned each day's lines only the night before – a necessity in many Hollywood productions because of constant script changes but a habit Hepburn considered lazy and unprofessional.) Whatever the reason, it's hard to believe in any emotional connection between the two stars.

Many critics caught the false notes in *The Rainmaker* but they were generally favourable anyway. The London *Observer* said her performance as "the plain unwanted woman who finds that it is within her own power to become both beautiful and desired again compels admiration for her qualities as an actress;" and Alton Cook called her "superb as she brings elderly barren despair to a blossoming of girlish bliss." She won another Oscar nomination but lost again, this time to Ingrid Bergman in *Anastasia.*

After Hepburn finished *The Rainmaker,* she and Tracy made *Desk Set.* Then she spent the summer of 1957 as a Guest Star at the American Shakespeare Festival in Stratford, Connecticut. Again she played Portia and she also appeared as Beatrice in *Much Ado About Nothing.* She toured with that play through the winter and following spring but after a bout of pneumonia on the road, she decided not to try to take it to Broadway. Instead, she went back to California to rest and relax – and read some film scripts.

She started her next picture in the spring of 1959, at the Shepperton Studios in England. She played the ghastly Violet Venable in *Suddenly, Last Summer,* based on the Tennessee Williams play with a screen adaptation by Gore Vidal. Hepburn found the subject matter objectionable but she recognized the dramatic impact of the play and she was willing to take on the challenge – particularly as she would be working again with Joseph Mankiewicz, who had produced *Woman Of The Year.* This time he was directing and Sam Spiegel,

A Long Day's Journey Into Night.

*The Lion In Winter.*

whom she knew from *The African Queen,* was the producer. Hepburn's co-stars were Elizabeth Taylor and Montgomery Clift.

*Suddenly, Last Summer* is a writer's *tour de force,* with a central character who never appears and a mysterious secret that, when finally revealed, actually manages to be truly astonishing. Mrs. Venable, recently bereaved by the loss of her son Sebastian, goes to an expensive mental sanatorium with her disturbed niece (Elizabeth Taylor) who keeps babbling about "dreadful things." Against the girl's strenuous objections, Mrs. Venable demands that her niece be given a lobotomy and even offers the hospital a million dollars as a sort of bribe. But the curious doctor gives the girl truth serum instead and she lets out the secret that Sebastian was a homosexual who was helped by his mother to procure lovers (she often forced her niece to act as a lure.) Sebastian's recent death on a North African beach is revealed to be due to a pack of street urchins, his sexual victims, turning on him in a grisly cannibalistic attack. When the doctor confronts Mrs. Venable with his knowledge, she goes over the edge of insanity.

Unconventional by any standards, the plot of *Suddenly, Last Summer* was a stunning surprise of 1959. Hepburn's role was particularly difficult since Violet Venable has to be a charming companion, a loving mother, a monster of depravity and quite insane – all at the same time. Moreover, her lines are mannered and highly artificial. It's hard to think of any other actress who could have conveyed the veneer of charm and the ruthless insanity underneath but Hepburn manages to make this unlikely character live.

But it was not a happy set. Mercedes McCambridge, who played Elizabeth Taylor's mother, remembers, "The ambiance and the vibrations were upsetting. I'm glad I wasn't in it more than I was. I was bitterly unhappy. Elizabeth was still mourning Mike Todd. Miss Hepburn was suffering through Spencer Tracy's illness. Albert Dekker died soon afterward. Joe (Mankiewicz) had something wrong with his hands – a skin disease – and he had to wear gloves all through the picture. I don't think you would think of Gore Vidal or Tennessee Williams as particularly happy people. Of course, Monty was in torment. Everybody connected with the film was going through some kind of personal anguish and it showed."

Hepburn was particularly concerned over the problems of Clift. He had not recovered from the automobile accident which had shattered his face and now, to the drugs he had been taking for years, he added others for the pain. The result was that it was hard for him to concentrate in long scenes and nearly impossible for him to remember his lines. Mankiewicz feared he was jeopardizing the whole production and wanted to fire him but Hepburn and Taylor banded together to insist that he be kept on. Hepburn was supportive to Clift as an actor and protective of him as a person and most people agree she got him through the movie. There is a story that when the shooting was over, Hepburn sought out Mankiewicz and spat in his face because she was so disapproving of his treatment of Clift.

Whatever the problems on the set, the film was a great success. It attracted large audiences and both Taylor and Hepburn received Academy Award nominations for their exceptionally good performances. Ironically,

*The Lion In Winter* – with Anthony Hopkins as her son, Richard the Lionheart.

*Guess Who's Coming To Dinner?* – Tracy died within weeks of finishing the film.

80

*Love Among The Ruins* with Laurence Olivier.

*Pat And Mike* – Hepburn and Tracy's last picture for MGM.

neither won and the Oscar went instead to Simone Signoret for *Room At The Top*. Many reviewers disliked the film: it was too static, too wordy, too improbable, too burdened with symbols and too consciously sensational. But Hepburn was generally congratulated for her work.

Hepburn did not work again until the fall of 1961 (perhaps the strain of that gloomy set had something to do with it) but chose instead to spend most of her time with the ailing Tracy. She was intrigued, however, when Ely Landau called her and told her he planned to make a film of the Eugene O'Neill play, *Long Day's Journey Into Night*. O'Neill wrote the largely autobiographical drama in 1940 but never showed it to anyone and stated in his will that it was not to be performed until 25 years after his death. However, his widow agreed to a Broadway production in 1956 and now Landau proposed to use the script without change for the movie. In fact, he did have to make a few cuts to bring the movie down to 174 minutes but no lines were changed or added. Suspecting that the film might not be a commercial success, Landau had a small budget of only $400,000 and Hepburn agreed to take a salary of just $25,000 (one-seventh of the salary for her previous picture.) The film was shot in a house on City Island, a little-known part of the Bronx, and work was completed in just thirty-seven days under the direction of Sidney Lumet.

*Long Day's Journey Into Night* is a look at the Tyrone family, one day in 1912, at their seaside cottage. The father (Ralph Richardson) is a selfish man who refuses to spend either the time or the money to help other members of the family. His wife Mary (Katharine Hepburn) is a secret drug-addict. Their older son (Jason Robards, Jr.) is somewhat sadistic and drinks too much. The younger son (Dean Stockwell) has tuberculosis and is about to be sent to a sanatorium. The drama centres on the relationships within this unhappy family: the love and loyalty; the cruelty, both intentional and thoughtless; the support and the exploitation.

It was another difficult part for Hepburn. Mary Tyrone is both self-pitying and self-destructive; she uses her misfortune as an excuse for failing to meet other people's needs and then asks them to feel sorry for her because of it; she has the sort of weakness that victimizes others. She is in fact the sort of person that Katharine Hepburn would dislike greatly if she met her in real life. But Hepburn managed to make Mary someone we understand even if we never like and someone we do feel sorry for, even though we see clearly that most of her troubles are of her own making.

There are those who believe it was her best performance and wherever one ranks it, its quality is unmistakeable. *Variety* said, "Katharine Hepburn's beautifully boned face mirrors her anguish and needs. She makes the role of mother breath-taking and intensely moving." Dwight Macdonald wrote of "that terrible smile, those suffering eyes;" Bosley Crowther called her "vibrant with hot and tragic truth, an eloquent representation of a lovely woman brought to feeble helpless ruin." She got another Academy Award nomination (her ninth) although she lost to Anne Bancroft in *The Miracle Worker*. And the film, as Ely Landau had feared, was not a success at the box office. Its distributor, Joseph E. Levine later cut an entire hour out of the movie but the drastically truncated version was no more successful.

Hepburn didn't make another film for five years, preferring to remain near Tracy whose health continued to fail. She emerged from her self-imposed retirement in the spring of 1967 to work with him in his last film, *Guess Who's Coming To Dinner,* for which she would win her third Oscar. Then came the shattering event of Tracy's death but within weeks, Hepburn was making plans for a number of new projects. The first to come to fruition was Martin Poll's production of *The Lion In Winter.*

James Goldman's play about Henry II and Eleanor of Aquitaine had been unsuccessful on Broadway several years before but Poll thought it could be a hit on the screen. He hired Anthony Harvey to direct and Peter O'Toole to play Henry. In the spring of 1968, Hepburn flew to London to start work. It was a congenial company (although Hepburn once slugged O'Toole for monopolizing the makeup man when she was waiting for him) and the shooting moved along swiftly, on location in Ireland and later, France.

Set in the twelfth century, *The Lion In Winter* tells the story of a royal family reunion. Henry II summons his elderly Queen from the confinement he has imposed on her and his three sons (John Castle, Anthony Hopkins, and Nigel Terry) to spend the Christmas holidays together and name a successor to his throne. The King of France (Timothy Dalton) and his sister (Jane Merrow) who is Henry's mistress, are also present. What follows is a sort of affectionate power struggle among parents and children, in which we see political manipulation to gain control of a powerful kingdom intertwined with gestures of familial love.

Here is Goldman's description of Eleanor of Aquitaine: "She is truly a handsome woman of great temperament, authority and presence. She has been a queen of international importance for 46 years and you know it. Finally, she is that most unusual thing: a genuinely feminine woman thoroughly capable of holding her own in a man's world." The role suggests something of Hepburn herself and it is a close match for her usual screen persona; Eleanor is obviously related to Tracy Lord, Tess Harding and Amanda Bonner. You can sense that Hepburn was glad to return to playing this sort of strong-willed clear-sighted character, after the string of tremulous victims that had occupied much of the 1960s.

Once again, her performance gained her an Academy Award nomination and to most people's surprise, she won it again. It was the culmination of a period of tremendous achievement for since 1951, she had made ten movies for which she received *seven* Academy Award nominations and won two Oscars. Most of the films were bix box office successes and all but one netted her reviews that ranged from good to ecstatic. It was an extraordinary period in an already extraordinary career.

*The Madwoman Of Chaillot* – a film version of Jean Giradoux's play.

# 7

# Recent Work

*In recent years, Hepburn has* continued her custom of moving back and forth between stage and screen and she's even added television dramas to her list of credits. Now in her seventies, she shows no signs of slowing down, either personally or professionally.

As soon as she finished shooting *The Lion In Winter,* she moved on to her next project, a movie version of Jean Giraudoux's play *The Madwoman Of Chaillot.* First performed in Paris in 1945, it ran on Broadway in 1949 with great success. John Huston was to direct its translation on to the screen and Ely Landau was the producer. An all-star cast was assembled including Charles Boyer, Yul Brynner, Edith Evans, Margaret Leighton, Danny Kaye, Richard Chamberlain, Nanette Newman – and more. But before filming started, Huston dropped out because he didn't like the way the script was shaping up. He was quite right on that point.

Bryan Forbes stepped in as director but he never managed to marshall the best efforts from his stars and the picture was an artistic failure. Much of the problem was indeed due to the script which mislaid the elements of timeless fantasy in an attempt to modernize the story. But some of the trouble is definitely due to Hepburn's interpretation of her role as Aurelia.

Hepburn plays the heroine, the Madwoman, an eccentric countess whose closest friends are streetpeople. Concluding that most human unhappiness is due to the greed of rich men, she hatches a plot to set a group of capitalists at one anothers' throats by convincing them that her house is sitting atop a gigantic oil field. (Nobody said this plot was logical.) To make this story work, Aurelia needs to be tough and determined, her craziness only a mask to    85 conceal her very sane view of the world but Hepburn plays her as a lovable old eccentric and that undermines the point. It's no longer a story of the clash between good and evil but a tale about a sentimental old woman stumbling across a way to thwart a few villains – almost the plot of a Disney TV movie. Most of the reviews were critical of this weakness and the picture was not a success.

When filming of *The Madwoman of Chaillot* was finished, Hepburn returned to New York to undertake a brand new project: a Broadway musical. It was *Coco,* based on the life of the French designer Chanel. Written by Alan Jay Lerner with music by Andre Previn, costumes and sets by Cecil Beaton and choreography by Michael Bennett, it was a first-rate production of a second-rate musical. Hepburn was not a singer in any conventional sense of the word but she croaked and whispered and shouted and murmured in time to the music and the effect was moving, if not strictly speaking musical. She carried a somewhat weak play and made it a success on Broadway from the minute it opened on December 18, 1969 until it closed on August 1 the following year. She later toured with it during the first half of 1971 and was nominated for a Tony but lost to Lauren Bacal in *Applause.*

In the months between the closing of the Broadway production andthe start of the tour, Hepburn went to Spain to shoot another film, *The Trojan Women.* It was a very personal film by Michael Cacoyannis who produced, directed and wrote the screen adaptation of the classical Greek tragedy. He assembled a powerful cast: in addition to Hepburn, he had Vanessa Redgrave, Genevieve Bujold and Irene Papas. Hepburn played Hecuba, aged queen of Troy and wife of Priam. She is the mother of Paris, whose kidnapping of the lovely Helen (Irene Papas) precipitates the Trojan War. The ruin this will bring on Troy is foreseen by Hecuba's daughter Cassandra (Genevieve Bujold) but her warnings are ignored. One of the casualties of the war is Hecuba's son Hector and he is mourned by his mother and wife (Vanessa Redgrave). With Hector dead, there is no warrior to save Troy, so it falls to the Greeks and Hecuba is given as a slave to Odysseus. The material is inherently dramatic but in this version it never quite came to life. *The Trojan Women* was not a box office success and the reviews were generally quite negative.

Hepburn's next project came in the spring of 1973, when she appeared in Edward Albee's play *A Delicate Balance* for Ely Landau's American Film Theater. This short-lived venture filmed plays and then showed them in movie houses to a subscription audience in an attempt to broaden the market for legitimate theatre. There was no attempt to make the movie anything other than a stage performance that happened to have been recorded on film. It was never a successful compromise and Hepburn was initially quite sceptical of the idea. She finally agreed, however, because she would have a chance to work opposite Paul Scofield and she also liked the choice of director, Tony Richardson. But she was not comfortable with the nastiness of Albee's characters – especially the one she played, the mother – and the whole performance never quite jelled.

Later that same year, Hepburn ventured into television with a made-for-TV version of *The Glass Menagerie,* the famous Tennessee Williams play about an aging Southern gentlewoman eroded by a lifetime of financial problems. Producer David Susskind had been after Hepburn for years to play

Coco – with music by **André** Previn, lyrics by Alan Jay Lerner and costumes by Cecil Beaton,
the play ran on Broadway for nine months.

*The Trojan Women* – Hepburn as Hecuba, Queen of Troy.

Amanda Wingfield and he finally got her to agree by promising that it would be shot just like a film and that she would have the help and support of a director she knew and respected, Anthony Harvey. The working conditions were thus ironed out but unfortunately, Hepburn was not really suited to the role she played. There is something stupid about Amanda's refusal to recognize the reality of her situation and Hepburn is never able to portray stupidity convincingly. The ratings for *The Glass Menagerie* were poor and the reviews were not much better.

Hepburn's next venture into television was altogether more successful. The vehicle was a sentimental little comedy called *Love Among The Ruins*. It was directed by George Cukor and it co-starred Sir Laurence Olivier. Set in the Edwardian period, it gave Hepburn the chance to wear a lot of fetching costumes and becoming feathery hats. *Love Among The Ruins* was a frothy confection with little substance – but only an old curmudgeon could insist on substance when confronted by the delicious spectacle of these two old monuments flirting so deftly. This time the ratings were fine and Hepburn won the television industry's award for excellence, the Emmy, for her performance.

It's certainly a comment on Hepburn's versatility that she could move from a successful appearance with Sir Laurence Olivier to an even more successful movie with John Wayne. This was *Rooster Cogburn*, shot on location in Oregon in the fall of 1974. The film was a sequel to *True Grit* for which Wayne had won an Oscar and it was a continuation of the adventures of the one-eyed marshal. In some ways the plot was a repeat of *The African Queen* with Hepburn playing a missionary whose father is killed by outlaws. Wayne rescues her from her isolated outpost and then together they track down the bad guys. Most of the movie is devoted to the adventure of the quest and, of course, the two incompatibles come to view one another first with respect and eventually with love.

Wayne was in declining health, having already lost a lung to cancer but he obviously enjoyed the picture. He said, "Rooster gives me a wonderful chance to play a character. Ordinarily, they just stand me up there and run everybody against me." He also enjoyed working with Hepburn. "I'd hate to think what this picture would be without her. She wants to do everything, too much really, because she can't ride worth a damn and I gotta keep reining in so she can keep up." But Hepburn was determined to do as much of her own stuntwork as possible. She commented, "I haven't waited all these years to do a cowboy picture with John Wayne to give up a single minute of it now." She also loved the Oregon wilderness where they were on location and she spent all her spare time shooting the rapids of the Rogue River in a little inflatable kayak (much to the horror of the company insuring the production.)

*Rooster Cogburn* was a success with the fans and the reviews were pleasant but it is clear by this stage of Hepburn's career (Wayne's as well, of course) that most critics were reviewing an institution rather than a particular performance by an actress. For example, Stanley Kaufman said, "How sensible not to put them in a sensible story, just to give them a romp that allows them to employ the personae they've constructed over more than 40 years," and concludes, "The more and longer you like stars, the more use they can make of your affection, for your pleasure."

In her next venture, Hepburn returned to the stage, starring in Enid Bagnold's play, *A Matter Of Gravity*. It opened on Broadway in February, 1976 and though the reviews for Hepburn were overwhelmingly favourable, most critics did not care for the play. Hepburn was cast as an elderly British eccentric living alone in a thirty room mansion whose grandson (Crhistopher Reeve) marries much to her distress, a Jamaican girl. After a lot of conversation about these and other topics, she decides to leave her home to her grandson and go to live in a private insane asylum – it's clear that the act is significant but not nearly so clear exactly what it signifies. However, Hepburn knows how to make eccentricity charming, if not particularly meaningful.

During rehearsals of the play, Hepburn fell going out of her front door and broke her hip. She was in a wheelchair for some time and says she now has an artificial hip. But there was no sign of disability in her movements during her next project, another made-for-TV movie, this time an adaptation of Emlyn Williams' play *The Corn Is Green*. It was shot in Wales, where the play is set, and Hepburn took long hikes in the Welsh countryside and rode her bicycle up and down the hilly roads.

Hepburn wrote a charming little piece for *TV Guide* about shooting *The Corn Is Green* saying she was happy to be working again with George Cukor who was directing and she liked and admired the young actor Ian Saynor who played the hero. Hepburn was comfortable in her part as a schoolmistress who encourages a talented boy from a mining family and intervenes to save his future when his girlfriend claims to be pregnant in order to force him into marriage. Ethel Barrymore played the part on Broadway, apparently as something of a *grande dame* and Bette Davis later starred in a film version. Hepburn's rendition was softer, warmer – perhaps a personal reflection of her interest in encouraging young actors (an interest of which Ian Saynor was then the beneficiary.)

Hepburn's next project was a film that has never been widely distributed. Intended primarily for children, it was called *Olly Olly Oxen Free* and starred Hepburn, two children and an English sheepdog. The quartet takes off on a string of adventures that culminates in a long balloon ride and an eventual descent into the middle of the Hollywood Bowl. Hepburn was 70 years old when she made this picture and it called for some strenuous and hazardous stunts. She insisted on doing them herself and willingly dangled in the air perched on an anchor suspended from the balloon as it travelled for miles across the California countryside. The film was not released until 1981, several years after it was made, and it never achieved much success.

Hepburn's next movie gave her the part – and the co-star – she had been waiting for. The part was Ethel Thayer, the co-star was Henry Fonda and the movie was *On Golden Pond*. It was an adaptation of a play by Ernest Thompson which Hepburn had seen in previews and according to the author, who also wrote the screenplay, "Hepburn wanted to do Ethel but said nothing about who as Norman. Henry wanted to play Norman but said nothing about who as Ethel. It was Jen (Fonda) who worked it all out." She bought the movie rights for her independent production company and then signed up her father and Hepburn. She decided to play the role of their daughter herself.

90

*Rooster Cogburn* – Hepburn's only film with John Wayne.

*On Golden Pond* was shot on location on a beautiful lake in New Hampshire. For the Fondas, it was something of a family reunion with Henry's wife and Jane's kids joining them there. Hepburn and Fonda had never met before the filming but they already respected each other's talent and they got on well together from the very first moment. Hepburn gave Fonda an old hat of Tracy's as a mark of her affection; deeply touched, Fonda responded by painting a picture of the hat and giving it to Hepburn. Hepburn said, "Working with Henry brings tears to my eyes. He is so sensitive, so giving an actor. I've always admired him, of course, but working with him for the first time is a marvel." Henry responded, "What a joy it is acting with Katharine. She can play all the levels of a scene and always is able to add something so fresh with a slight gesture or look."

The screenplay follows the play closely. It is the story of a family coming to terms with the passage of time. Norman, a somewhat acerbic personality, is showing symptoms of failing health and he is becoming forgetful. His wife Ethel is painfully aware of these signs of mortality but tries not to let it spoil present happiness as they spend another summer on the lake they have always loved. Their daughter Chelsea comes to visit, bringing her resentment over unresolved conflicts with her father. Her mother scolds her for her persistence in holding on to the misery of the past and Chelsea says vaguely she hopes sometime she and her father will become friends. Ethel responds tartly, "Chelsea, Norman is 80 years old. He has heart palpitations and a problem remembering things. When exactly do you expect this friendship to begin?" But of course, by the end of the picture, it does begin, as does a special relationship between Norman and Chelsea's stepson (Doug McKeon). The family will be able to treasure the memory of one last wonderful summer on Golden Pond.

Both fans and critics received *On Golden Pond* warmly. Undoubtedly, part of the reason was sentimentality. Fonda at 75 was known to be in frail health, using a pacemaker to keep his own heart going and the knowledge added special poignancy to the scenes in which Norman experiences heart trouble. And it was known that Fonda's real-life daughter had gone through a period of estrangement from him that mirrored the problems of Norman and Chelsea – another tug at the heartstrings. One can't escape the suspicion that both Hepburn and Fonda were praised simply because they are among the increasingly rare survivors of our shared cinematic past. But beyond all the sentiment lies the plain unadorned fact that both stars *did* turn in good performances and that the movie was affecting and touching. It came as no suprise when both leads were nominated for an Academy Award – and no surprise either when they both won: Fonda for the first time, Hepburn for the fourth.

But long before the nominations were announced, Hepburn had moved on to her next project, starring in Ernest Thompson's new play, *The West Side Waltz*. Undoubtedly written with Hepburn in mind, it is the story of an elderly widow living alone, who must learn at last to admit and accept her dependence on other people. The stages of the heroine's acceptance of this dependence are almost sadistically linked to the stages of her physical deterioration: she starts the play with a slight arthritic limp and progresses scene by scene to a cane, then a walker, a wheelchair and then fianlly to confinement to the sofa. There is more than an echo of earlier Hepburn heroines who had to admit their weaknesses, or in some way be brought low before they could release their humanity. Here the function of Spencer Tracy is played by Father Time – but the humiliation seems as brutal as the worst of the Tracy-Hepburn plots.

*The West Side Waltz* opened on Broadway in November, 1981, and its reception was very similar to that of *A Matter Of Gravity*. There were complaints about the play but universal praise for Hepburn and she drew packed houses until it closed in March of 1982. At the time of writing, the play is on the road and continues to do very well – Hepburn as usual pulls big crowds everywhere. There are no hints as to what her next project might be when this play finally closes.

*On Golden Pond* – with Jane Fonda.

94

*Keeper Of The Flame.*

# 8

# A Jury of Her Peers

*In a film career that has spanned* more than 50 years, Hepburn has had as leading men most of the great stars of our time: John Barrymore, Robert Taylor, Sir Laurence Olivier, John Wayne, Douglas Fairbanks, Jr., Peter O'Toole, Henry Fonda, Sir Ralph Richardson, Humphrey Bogart, Cary Grant – the list goes on and on. She has also worked with many well-respected film directors, such as Cukor and Stevens, Hawks and Capra, Minelli and Huston. And she has worked with hundreds of the top professionals behind the cameras: Walter Plunkett, Irene and Adrian for costumes; Cedric Gibbons and Oliver Messel for sets; Claude Renoir, Jack Cardiff, Jack Hildyard on camera; a long list of distinguished writers creating the story and many of the best-known producers. It is these fellow workers whose opinions of Hepburn as an actress are best informed and most interesting.

At the beginning of her career, there were those who criticized her sharply. On the set of her first film, during a disagreement with her co-star John Barrymore, Hepburn said angrily, "I'll never play another scene with you," and he shot back suavely, "But, my dear, you never have." Much of the criticism of Hepburn as an actress in those early days focused on her tendency to overact. When Jed Harris directed her in *The Lake,* he was particularly harsh in his judgement on that count. "I could see she was hopeless. I fought with her – I begged her to stop posing, striking attitudes, leaning against doorways, putting a limp hand to her forehead, to stop being a big movie star and *feel* the lines, *feel* the character. It was trying the impossible, to make an artificial showcase for an artificial star . . . Tremendous artificiality! It's as though she had seen her own performance and liked her own rather charming babbling at everything and she

95

had decided that was acting."

Of course, Jed Harris had his reasons for stating the case so unkindly. But George Cukor, who likes and admires Hepburn and has elicited some of her very best performances, put much the same criticism in a gentler way. Speaking of *Keeper Of The Flame,* he said, "It was Kate's last romantic glamour-girl part and she acted with some of that artificiality she supposedly left behind at RKO . . . I didn't like the 'glamour' side of Kate; I loved the fresh natural Kate when she forgot to be a movie queen. The subject brought out the movie queen in her and that wasn't good."

Several people suggested that part of the problem might have been that she hadn't yet learned the techniques of acting for the screen. John Cromwell, who directed the lamentable *Spitfire,* said, "I realized she was instinctively a very good actress but she had never taken the trouble to learn more about the business." And George Stevens, who directed Hepburn in *Alice Adams,* later said, "I never knew an actress of whom I was surer as to potentiality but I never knew an actress of whom I was less sure that the promise would come through. She not only had no technique, she didn't seem to want any."

Hepburn's best performances have come from working with directors who have helped her combat this problem of occasional overacting and artificiality. Stevens taught her to be quiet, to let things sometimes happen to her instead of always having to be the agent. He said, "She had always thought that to play a love scene with a man involved standing up straight and talking to him strong, eye to eye. I made her have confidence in her beauty, so that if she sat in a chair, letting her head fall back, with a wide-brimmed hat over her eyes, she had a quiet assurance she was attracting her man; she didn't have to bulldoze him into submission." Although Hepburn continued to play many roles that required the kind of aggressiveness Stevens was talking about, she did in fact learn to let her heroines fall into quieter, more responsive moods.

Of course, Hepburn has always been a thinking actress. Gregory LaCava, director of *Stage Door,* commented, "She is completely the intellectual actress. She has to understand the why of everything before she can feel; then, when the meaning has soaked in, emotion comes — and superb work." Her artistic failures happened when the emotion never came. In fact, it seems likely that in the early part of her career, the defences she maintained in most of her relationships with people other than her family may have limited her emotional experiences as a person and thus her emotional range as an actress. For some of her parts, she simply didn't yet have enough to draw on.

But despite all the criticism, most colleagues agreed even then that she had some magical quality that came alive in front of the camera — a vitality and zest, a glow, that made her attract the viewer's attention always. Lucille Ball noticed it during the shooting of *Stage Door:* "Everytime she gets into a new scene, no matter where, or on what stage, and she's wearing a new outfit, every son-of-a-bitch on this lot finds his way, or her way over there to stand around and gawk. Why is that? Don't ask me but they sure all want to look at her and watch her and see what she does. I do it myself. And the grips from the other sets and cutters and messengers and readers. They all find their way and stand around taking her in like out-of-town visitors."

*Little Women* – with Edna May Oliver.

*The African Queen.*

Cukor put it his way, when he directed her first film, *Bill Of Divorcement.* "This odd creature had her own grace, her own style. I was excited by her. Her face moved correctly for the screen, it had a light, a radiance . . . Kate was quite good in rehearsals but she didn't really come alive until the camera closed in on her. I had a rough idea she was doing well but she sprang to life when I saw the rushes. Her odd awkwardness, her odd shifts of emphasis, these were proof of her being alive on the screen. She wasn't too smooth, she was fresh." Colin Clive, her co-star in her second picture, said, "She is not just a face but a terrific personality. She is not beautiful . . . though she understands the art of acting so amazingly that she can convey the illusion of beauty if the part demands it."

On a personal level, most of her professional colleagues got on well with Hepburn. They recognized and respected her determination and her enormous willingness to work. Frances Dee, who played one of the March sisters in *Little Women,* remembers, "She was always the first on the set every day, lines perfect, glowing with health, and never the slightest sign of temperament." Walter Plunkett commented on another aspect of her thoroughness. "She accepted her costumes as things she would normally put on every morning. They were *not* costumes, they were the clothes she wore."

Hepburn was also known to be very supportive of other actors. Cary Grant credits her with valuable help in encouraging him into the comedy roles at which he was to excel. John Beal, Hepburn's relatively unknown co-star in *The Little Minister,* remembers that during the shooting of one scene, "I was very respectful; too much, probably. I would bend over backward to obscure myself. She felt I was underplaying and she drew me aside and said, 'Don't be afraid to do things on your own.'"

She fussed over her co-stars' health as well as their careers. Partly out of a concern for her fellow workers' nutrition, she inaugurated a custom during the filming of *Little Women* that she followed on most of her films thereafter. Every day she brought a big picnic lunch to which she invited all the cast and crew. Cukor admits that he thought at first it was an affectation but then he saw how it worked to draw people together, to make them feel like a unit and he was soon a whole-hearted supporter of the tradition.

Comments made by colleagues who first worked with Hepburn later in her career indicate something about her growth as an actress. It seems obvious that over the years she learned to be less theatrical and more natural, to be more economical with gesture and business and to let her emotions take their place alongside her intellect. Cukor had something to do with this, as did George Stevens, another director with whom she made several films. Playing comedy may also have taught her restraint, as in the case of *Bringing Up Baby,* where she had to learn to let the audience find the laugh instead of leading them to it or demanding it from them. Perhaps her very best teacher was Spencer Tracy; she definitely seems to have caught something from his low-key naturalism. Stanley Kramer remembers watching this learning going on, even in their last film together. "We'd be rehearsing and she'd suddenly come in and kneel down alongside him. She was always watching the camera angle (for her neck, about which she was very sensitive) and she liked to be low down. So he'd look at her and say, 'What the hell are you doing down there?' And she'd say, 'Well, Spence, I just thought . . .' He'd say, 'You just thought. You always talk as though you'd got a feather in your anus. Now for God's sake get up out of there and let's do what the feller wants to do. Come in like a normal human being.' And she'd do it.''

Of the mature Hepburn, Tennesse Williams wrote in praise, ''Kate is a playwright's dream actress. She makes dialogue sound better than it is by a matchless beauty and clarity of diction, and by a fineness of intelligence and sensibility that illuminates every shade of meaning in every line she speaks. She invests every scene, each bit, with the intuition of an artist born into her part.'' Ian Saynor said after working with her in *The Corn Is Green*, ''She was so professional, so committed to that job and a very, very thoughtful actress – somebody who'd worry about what she was doing and why she'd be doing it. Sometimes she could just turn and look at you – and knock you off your feet, because you're not expecting that kind of power. She would be so powerful, so compelling, that you really had to respond if you'd got any sort of emotional feelings or anything inside you. You can't help but react to somebody doing what she does – it's really incredible.''

Cukor, who directed Hepburn and Saynor, had additional thoughts that underscore Hepburn's increasing emotional directness and power. ''She surprised me in every scene. She has such freshness and spontaneity. She never goes for the obvious effect. It might have been done rather heavily, rather worthily, but in her case the seriousness is underneath, concealed in warmth, humanity and tolerance. She doesn't soften the blow but she also has a kind of joy and gaiety that is irresistible and never becomes routine. And she plays it with more understanding than she would have thirty years ago.''

Robert Morley, who played her brother in *The African Queen*, remarked particularly on her technical competence. ''She knew a good deal more about the business than I did. She was the sort of lady who, when you were doing a scene with her and you weren't very clever about getting into the right position or were about to fall over one of the cables, would continue with her performance, impeccably, and at the same time manage to push you into the right place with a friendly shove and pick up the cable as well!'' Stanley Kramer paid tribute to Hepburn's enormous attention to detail while she was working. ''Kate contributes to everything. She's got something to say about the words, about the costumes, the camera angle, the lighting, the camera man, the dress designer, everything, every minute detail. The ashtrays on the table, the way a lamp is connected.''

It seems that increasing stature in the film industry has not created any change in Hepburn's co-operative attitude toward her fellow actors. Bogart commented, ''She's actually kind of sweet and lovable. And she's absolutely honest and absolutely fair about her work. None of this late on the set or demanding close-ups . . . She doesn't have to be waited on, either. You never pull up a chair for Kate. You tell her, ''Kate, pull up a chair, willya, and while you're at it, get one for yourself.''' Alfred Drake, with whom she appeared on stage in *Much Ado About Nothing,* said, ''She was kind, thoughtful, generous to the other players. She never upstaged the young girls or pushed them out of the limelight.

She was always present thirty minutes before everyone else and always the last to leave. She was an inspiration to everyone, an ideal team worker."

Perhaps director Anthony Harvey summed it all up best: "Working with her is like going to Paris at the age of 17 and finding everything is the way you thought it would be." What other actress could so well live up to the illusion she has created?

Alec Guinness visits the set of *Suddenly, Last Summer*.

*Sea Of Grass* – with Melvyn Douglas.

# 9

# A Twentieth Century Image of Woman

Unquestionably, Katharine Hepburn has become a twentieth-century icon. Certain images of her are fixed in our culture – indeed, they have *become* our culture. Hepburn as Tracy Lord, in tailored slacks and a severe black blouse, hands on her hips, cheekbones jutting, a flinty look in her eye and a general attitude that convinces you she will take no prisoners. Hepburn as Amanda Bonner, wearing a succession of coldly stylish suits to do battle in the courtroom where she has the witnesses, the judge, the jury and her own husband in awe of her cutting competence and her willingness to go to any extremes to win. Hepburn as Tess Harding, perched on the edge of a desk in a cluttered newspaper office, shooting Spencer Tracy a murderously challenging look as he enters her territory. Hepburn as Sydney Fairfield watching the progression of her father's madness that spells the ruin of all her hopes, with that clear, candid unflinching gaze. And of course, Hepburn as Sylvia Scarlett, dressed as a boy in well-cut flannels, a snap-brimmed hat temporarily covering her short-short haircut.

These images have both reflected and stimulated changes in the way we look at women. When Hepburn first appeared on the screen in the early 1930s, she seemed to be virtually her own original creation. As George Cukor put it, "She was like nobody we'd ever seen, for better or worse." What other female star displayed that alarming directness and that seeming lack of coquetry that became her trademark? Vincent Canby calls her physical presence "a fusion of long lithe body with grace of movement and an intelligence that can be as scratchy as sandpaper . . ."

Even (or perhaps especially) in her love scenes, Hepburn never

104

Reading the script of *Guess Who's Coming To Dinner?*

seemed to soften or yield. The Hepburn heroine in love was disdainful of feminine wiles; if she played any game, it was likely to be a straightforward round of golf in which she trounced her male companion. Using gestures more frequently associated with men than women – breaking a golf club over her knee, for example, in *The Philadelphia Story*, she always looked and acted as if she were in total control of the situation. And the man.

Pauline Kael summed up the impact of Hepburn's screen image most succinctly: "At her best – in the archetypal Hepburn role as the tomboy Linda in *Holiday* in 1938 – her wit and nonconformity made ordinary heroines seem mushy, and her angular beauty made the round-faced ingenues look piggy and stupid. She was hard where they were soft – both in head and body." And the screen image was reinforced by the public picture of the private person. She always wore pants and severely tailored jackets and coats. Although she admitted she was married, her husband was virtually invisible and obviously exerted not the least bit of control over her existence. Single again, she never went out on "dates" like other stars and when she did have a love affair, as with Howard Hughes, it was he who followed her around the country as she stuck to her professional commitments. And in interviews, she was always outspoken in her belief that marriage and motherhood were not appropriate occupations for her. She was as dedicated to her work as any man and she had no male manager in the background making all her decisions for her. She often found and sometimes even financed her own projects and there were many stories about her ability to drive a hard bargain with tough studio execs.

The total image was that of an independent woman. Hepburn stood on her own, made her own individual way in the world, and insisted that men had to accept her as an equal. At least, that was the view most people had, especially in the 1930s and '40s. But the more closely you look at the Hepburn persona, the more you must conclude that this presumed independence was all style and no substance.

In actual fact, her clashes with the men in her life usually resulted in a clear loss for Hepburn. She had to fix breakfast in bed for her growling mate (*Women Of The Year*) or begin to broadcast a political speech that offended her deepest convictions (*State Of The Union*) or resort to suicide (*Christopher Strong*). Over and over again, she must admit that she has Gone Too Far. Then, humbled and humiliated, she takes her rightful place under the thumb of her man. The fact that, as in *Adam's Rib*, she may continue to make some verbal jabs, only emphasizes that they are nothing more than a style, a mannerism, a way of showing some becoming spunk. They are not a sign of her genuine equality but a foible that her man is secure enough to permit.

This principle seemed to apply as well in the publicly visible aspects of her private life. Below the verbal sparring with Tracy lay a very traditional relationship. She went on location with him, nursed him through his bouts of drinking and eventual failing health, learned to fix strong coffee and rare steaks the way he liked them, and even quit working altogether for a number of years at the peak of her career in order to be with him. There are no signs of equivalent sacrifices on his part. And her interviews all indicate an assumption that this state of affairs is satisfactory, even enviable.

It is interesting to note how frequently it happens that once Hepburn's feelings of romance (often rather high-minded and never overtly sexual) have been declared, there seems to be no need for the further presence of the man involved. Generally, the movie ends before there is any physical or domestic involvement. Although the Hepburn heroine could not be called asexual, there is never a sense that sex creates a bond between her and the hero; she always seems to be above mere matters of the flesh. Hepburn heroines can even manage to be married without the usual concommitant of having a husband present (echoing her private life.) In *State Of The Union* and *Sea Of Grass,* the husband is estranged for most of the picture; in *Without Love,* his status is purely Platonic. It is a rare Hepburn movie in which daily cohabitation takes place, and when it does – in *Woman Of The Year* and *Adam's Rib,* for example – the marriage is in trouble. In her later years, she did make two movies (*Guess Who's Coming To Dinner* and *On Golden Pond*) that postulated an ordinary domestic existence but even these feature no visible responsibility for running, or making a home. The point is, in order to retain her integrity and her highly-valued independent stance, the Hepburn character must forego any genuine commitment or responsibility to an ongoing partnership.

If the Hepburn heroine is reluctant to become a wife in any usual sense of the word, she is even more reluctant to become a mother, thus escaping that other great bond most women must manage. In *Christopher Strong,* it might be said that she goes so far as to choose death over motherhood. In *Woman Of The Year,* she turns motherhood into a travesty by adopting a Greek orphan rather than bearing Spencer Tracy's child. If children are for some reason a necessary adjunct to the plot, as in *State Of The Union,* they are simply trotted in by a servant and whisked away again. Later on in her career, Hepburn did eventually play roles in which motherhood was a more central aspect of character. But these are terrible warnings of the harm mothers can do rather than maternal models to follow. Violet Venable – incestuously doting, utterly depraved, finally mad; or Mary Tyrone – weakness made tyrannical to rob her children of their own strength: these are mothers gone amok.

The conclusion seems to be that there is no way to incorporate motherhood into the Hepburn version of the independent woman. One has ony to think of a star who came along twenty years later, Doris Day, to realize what an extreme point of view the Hepburn heroine embodies. Day also played the part of a career-minded woman, heading off for the office in a succession of stylish suits. She's good at her work, often defined by it. She challenges male authority in conflicts with her boss and arguments with the hero. But sooner or later she's surrounded by a bevy of children and a dog or two, living with her hero-husband in daily domestic exchange. Certainly there are many aspects of unreality about the character Day plays but at least she recognizes the existence of a husband and children and the need to be involved with them.

Another human relationship that the Hepburn heroine seems to eschew is friendship. She never has a female confidante or sidekick. Even in a movie like *Stage Door,* with its almost dormitory-like feeling of girls wearing one another's clothes, swapping dates, creating a network of mutual support against the difficult world outside their door, Hepburn is portrayed as a threateningly

Overleaf: Between scenes on *The World And His Wife.*

independent outsider. It's impossible to imagine her trying on Lucille Ball's blouse or giggling over a double date with Eve Arden. If Hepburn does have a friend on screen, she seems to exist for the express purpose of being cut out, as in the case of the unfortunate Hilary in *Guess Who's Coming To Dinner*. After an unspecified number of years of friendship and business association, Hilary is exiled for a couple of remarks she made in the first thirty seconds of shock after learning that her friend's daughter was about to marry a black man. Our image of 'Hepburn the Friend' is that of the avenging angel, casting Hilary out of paradise with an imperious gesture. And even that is more of a relationship that she typically seems to have with other women. Generally, they are simply foils against which her originality is shown to its best advantage – those ingenues that she makes look piggy and stupid.

In fact, the only relationships that Hepburn ever succeeds in sustaining on the screen are those with members of her family. Here she excels. She is fond of her mother in *Bill Of Divorcement*, close to her parents and sisters in *Little Women*, resolutely attached to her disgraced dad in *Sylvia Scarlett*, solicitous of her brother's welfare in *Holiday*, protective of her mother in *The Philadelphia Story*, devoted to her father in *Undercurrent*, and so on. This suggests an essentially adolescent quality about the Hepburn persona. The image – a successful daughter and sister who has not yet learned to manage the more demanding, threatening or engulfing role of wife and mother – reflects the feelings and concerns of a teenage girl rather than an adult woman.

We end up with a curious paradox. Based on the conjunction of her screen roles and her public image, Hepburn has come to represent the independent woman to generations of movie-goers. And it is not just the women who saw her on the screen in the Thirties and Forties who think of her that way. Even Jane Fonda, that symbol of liberated consciousness, is on record as being in awe of the Hepburn legend of independence and intimates that she is trying to live up to the older woman's example. But in truth, Hepburn's movies, as well as certain aspects of her personal myth, emphasize a very traditional point of view, based on concepts of male dominance and female submission. The Hepburn heroine is liberated only because she has escaped all of the ties that bind. She is in control of her life only when she is alone in the room.

Perhaps this reflects something about the cultural assumptions of the decades of the 1930s and 1940s, when she rose to public prominence and established her image and legend. The style of an independent woman was startling enough at that time; the substance might have been insupportable. A woman who was genuinely beyond the reach of male dominance, who really saw herself as the central figure in the drama of existence, like Mae West, had to camouflage the fact behind a style of traditional femininity exaggerated almost to the level of parody. Only a woman like the Hepburn heroine, whose life fell so completely within the confines of the traditional assumptions about a woman's role, could get away with the appearance of independence. The hardness, the abrasiveness of this woman's style could then be seen as mere feminine provocation. But of course the acceptance of the style inevitably paved the way for further change and it is not surprising that a generation of young women brought up to admire the style should begin to pursue the substance.

But there may be a deeper truth underlying the paradox of the Hepburn heroine, with implications that go beyond the questions of our attitudes toward the position of women and point up a factor central to our current culture. Again and again, we see that Hepburn must ahieve her position of independence by sacrificing most ordinary human relationships. It's the true American definition of independence: being alone. As the song puts it, "Freedom's just another word for nothing left to lose," but it is this adolescent, egotistical version of freedom that is continually celebrated in our culture of individualism. Tracy Lord's icy independence is simply the female version of Shane riding off alone to Somewhere Else. Both speak of the desire to be free and the assumption that love and intimacy mitigate against freedom. The ultimate outcome of a commitment to the cult of the individual and his or her freedom is isolation.

Perhaps it's true that love and freedom are incompatible. Or perhaps it's just the sterile interpretation we have of freedom. In either case, it seems clear that Katharine Hepburn speaks to some yearning to stand above the ties of daily life, to be wholly individual, to be beyond the reach of the ordinary problems of relationships between man and women. Hepburn is one of those rare figures who both reflects our sense of ourselves and, through her extraordinary vividness and clarity, contributes to it. For half a century, she has represented an important aspect of the twentieth-century image of womankind.

*State Of The Union* – front of house still showing the film's UK title.

*On Golden Pond* – with Henry Fonda.

# 10

## Filmography

A BILL OF DIVORCEMENT
RKO 1932
Director: George Cukor
Producer: David O. Selznick
Screenplay: Howard Estabrook and Harry Wagstaff Gribble, based on the play by Clemence Dane
Cast: John Barrymore, Billie Burke, Katharine Hepburn, David Manners

CHRISTOPHER STRONG
RKO 1933
Director: Dorothy Arzner
Producer: David O. Selznick
Screenplay: Zoe Akins, based on a novel by Gilbert Frankau
Cast: Katharine Hepburn, Colin Clive, Billie Burke, Helen Chandler, Ralph Forbes

MORNING GLORY
RKO 1933
Director: Lowell Sherman
Producer: Pandro S. Berman
Screenplay: Howard J. Green, based on a play by Zoe Akins
Cast: Katharine Hepburn, Douglas Fairbanks, Jr., Adolphe Menjou, Mary Duncan, C. Aubrey Smith

LITTLE WOMEN
RKO 1933
Director: George Cukor
Producer: Merian C. Cooper
Screenplay: Sarah Y. Mason and Victor Heerman, based on the novel by Louisa May Alcott
Cast: Katharine Hepburn, Joan Bennett, Paul Lukas, Edna May Oliver, Jean Parker, Frances Dee, Henry Stephenson, Douglass Montgomery, Spring Byington

SPITFIRE
RKO 1934
Director: John Cromwell
Producer: Merian C. Cooper
Screenplay: Jane Murfin and Lula Vollmer, based on a play by Lula Vollmer
Cast: Katharine Hepburn, Robert Young, Ralph Bellamy

THE LITTLE MINISTER
RKO 1934
Director: Richard Wallace
Producer: Pandro S. Berman
Screenplay: Jane Murfin, Sarah Y. Mason and Victor Heerman (additional scenes by Mortimer Offner and Jack Wagner) based on the novel and play by Sir James M. Barrie
Cast: Katharine Hepburn, John Beal, Alan Hale, Donald Crisp, Lumsden Hare, Dorothy Stickney

BREAK OF HEARTS
RKO 1935
Director: Philip Mueller
Producer: Pandro S. Berman
Screenplay: Sarah Y. Mason, Victor Heerman and Anthony Veiller, based on a story by Lester Cohen
Cast: Katharine Hepburn, Charles Boyer, John Beal, Jean Hersholt (Jason Robards in a bit part)

ALICE ADAMS
RKO 1935
Director: George Stevens
Producer: Pandro S. Berman
Screenplay: Dorothy Yost and Mortimer Offner, based on the novel by Booth Tarkington
Cast: Katharine Hepburn, Fred MacMurray, Fred Stone, Evelyn Venable, Frank Albertson, Grady Sutton, Hedda Hopper, Hattie McDaniel

SYLVIA SCARLETT
RKO 1936
Director: George Cukor
Producer: Pandro S. Berman
Screenplay: Gladys Unger, John Collier and Mortimer Offner,
based on a novel by Compton MacKenzie
Cast: Katharine Hepburn, Cary Grant, Brian Aherne, Edmund
Gwenn, Natalie Paley

MARY OF SCOTLAND
RKO 1936
Director: John Ford
Producer: Pandro S. Berman
Screenplay: Dudley Nichols, based on the play by Maxwell
Anderson
Cast: Katharine Hepburn, Fredric March, Florence Eldridge,
Douglas Walton, John Carradine, Robert Barrat, Gavin Muir, Alan
Mowbray, Donald Crisp, Anita Colby

A WOMAN REBELS
RKO 1936
Director: Mark Sandrich
Producer: Pandro S. Berman
Screenplay: Anthony Veiller and Ernest Vajda, based on a novel
by Netta Syrett
Cast: Katharine Hepburn, Herbert Marshall, Elizabeth Allan,
Donald Crisp, Doris Dudley, Van Heflin

QUALITY STREET
RKO 1937
Director: George Stevens
Producer: Pandro S. Berman
Screenplay: Mortimer Offner and Allan Scott, based on the play
by Sir James M. Barrie
Cast: Katharine Hepburn, Franchot Tone, Fay Bainter, Eric Blore,
Cora Witherspoon, Estelle Winwood, Florence Lake, Helena
Grant, Bonita Granville (Joan Fontaine in a bit part)

STAGE DOOR
RKO 1937
Director: Gregory LaCava
Producer: Pandro S. Berman
Screenplay: Morris Ryskind and Anthony Veiller, based on the
play by Edna Ferber and George S. Kaufman
Cast: Katharine Hepburn, Adolphe Menjou, Ginger Rogers, Gail
Patrick, Constance Collier, Andrea Leeds, Lucille Ball, Franklin
Pangborn, Grady Sutton, Jack Carson, Eve Arden, Ann Miller

BRINGING UP BABY
RKO 1938
Director & Producer: Howards Hawks
Screenplay: Dudley Nichols and Hagar Wilde, based on a story by
Hagar Wilde
Cast: Katharine Hepburn, Cary Grant, Charles Ruggles, May
Robson, Walter Catlett, Barry Fitzgerald, Fritz Feld, Asta, Nissa,
Jack Carson, Ward Bond

HOLIDAY
Columbia 1938
Director: George Cukor
Producer: Everett Riskin
Screenplay: Donald Ogden Stewart and Sidney Buchman, based
on the play by Philip Barry
Cast: Katharine Hepburn, Cary Grant, Doris Nolan, Lew Ayres,
Edward Everett Horton, Henry Kolker, Binnie Barnes, Jean Dixon,
Henry Daniell

THE PHILADELPHIA STORY
Metro-Goldwyn-Mayer 1940
Director: George Cukor
Producer: Joseph L. Mankiewiez
Screenplay: Donald Ogden Stewart, based on the play by Philip
Barry
Cast: Cary Grant, Katharine Hepburn, James Stewart, Ruth
Hussey, John Howard, Roland Young, John Halliday

WOMAN OF THE YEAR
Metro-Goldwyn-Mayer 1942
Director: George Stevens
Producer: Joseph L. Mankiewiez
Screenplay: Ring Lardner, Jr. and Michael Kanin
Cast: Spencer Tracy, Katharine Hepburn, Fay Bainter, Reginald
Owen, Minor Watson, William Bendix, Gladys Blake

KEEPER OF THE FLAME
Metro-Goldwyn-Mayer 1942
Director: George Cukor
Producer: Victor Saville
Screenplay: Donald Ogden Stewart, based on the novel by I.A.R.
Wylie
Cast: Spencer Tracy, Katharine Hepburn, Richard Whorf,
Margaret Wycherly, Donald Meek, Forrest Tucker, Percy Kilbride,
Howard Da Silva, Darryl Hickman

STAGE DOOR CANTEEN
Sol Lesser Production United Artists 1943
Director: Frank Borzage
Producer: Sol Lesser
Screenplay: Delmer F. Daves
Cast: Cheryl Walker, William Terry, Marjorie Riordan (Ruth Roman in a bit part). Cameo apearances by stars too numerous to mention, including: Judith Anderson, Tallulah Bankhead, Ray Bolger, Katherine Cornell, Helen Hayes, Katharine Hepburn, Gertrude Lawrence, Gypsy Rose Lee, Harpo Marx, Yehudi Menuhin, Merle Oberon, George Raft, Johnny Weissmuller, Ed Wynn

DRAGON SEED
Metro-Goldwyn-Mayer 1944
Director: Jack Conway and Harold S. Bucquet
Producer: Pandro S. Berman
Screenplay: Marguerite Robbins and Jane Murfin, based on the novel by Pearl S. Buck
Cast: Katharine Hepburn, Walter Huston, Aline MacMahon, Akim Tamiroff, Turhan Bey, Hurd Hatfield, Frances Raffert, Agnes Moorhead, J. Carrol Nash (Lionel Barrymore as the narrator)

WITHOUT LOVE
Metro-Goldwyn-Mayer 1945
Director: Harold S. Bucquet
Producer: Lawrence A. Weingarten
Screenplay: Donald Ogden Stewart, based on the play by Philip Barry
Cast; Spencer Tracy, Katharine Hepburn, Lucille Ball, Keenan Wynn, Carl Esmond

UNDERCURRENT
Metro-Goldwyn-Mayer 1946
Director: Vincente Minelli
Producer: Pandro S. Berman
Screenplay: Edward Chodorov, based on a story by Thelma Strabel
Cast: Katharine Hepburn, Robert Taylor, Robert Mitchum, Edmund Gwenn, Marjorie Main, Jayne Meadows

THE SEA OF GRASS
Metro-Goldwyn-Mayer 1947
Director: Elia Kazan
Producer: Pandro S. Berman
Screenplay: Marguerite Roberts and Vincent Lawrence, based on 117

the novel by Conrad Richter
Cast: Katharine Hepburn, Spencer Tracy, Melvyn Douglas,
Phyllis Thaxter, Robert Walker, Harry Carey

SONG OF LOVE
Metro-Goldwyn-Mayer 1947
Director & Producer: Clarence Brown
Screenplay: Ivan Tors, Irmgard Von Cube, Allen Vincent and
Robert Ardrey, based on the play by Bernard Schubert and Mario
Silva
Cast: Katharine Hepburn, Paul Henreid, Robert Walker, Henry
Daniell, Leo G. Carroll

STATE OF THE UNION
Liberty Film Production/Metro-Goldwyn-Mayer 1948
Director & Producer: Frank Capra
Screenplay: Anthony Veiller and Myles Connolly, based on the
play by Howard Lindsay and Russell Crouse
Cast: Spencer Tracy, Katharine Hepburn, Van Johnson, Angela
Lansbury, Adolphe Menjou, Lewis Stone, Howard Smith,
Margaret Hamilton

ADAM'S RIB
Metro-Goldwyn-Mayer 1949
Director: George Cukor
Producer: Lawrence Weingarten
Screenplay: Garson Kanin and Ruth Gordon
Cast: Spencer Tracy, Katharine Hepburn, Judy Holliday, Tom
Ewell, David Wayne, Jean Hagen, Hope Emerson

THE AFRICAN QUEEN
Horizon Romulus Production/United Artists (in Technicolor)
1951
Director: John Huston
Producer: S.P. Eagle
Screenplay: James Agee and John Huston, based on the novel by
C.S. Forester
Cast: Humphrey Bogart, Katharine Hepburn, Robert Morley,
Peter Bull, Theodore Bikel

PAT AND MIKE
Metro-Goldwyn-Mayer 1952
Director: George Cukor
Producer: Lawrence Weingarten
Screenplay: Garson Kanin and Ruth Gordon
Cast: Spencer Tracy, Katharine Hepburn, Aldo Ray, William
Ching, Sammy White, George Mathews, Charles Buchinski (now
Bronson), Jim Backus, Chuck Connors

SUMMERTIME
Lopert Film Production/United Artists (in Technicolor) 1955
Director: David Lean
Producer: Ilya Lopert
Screenplay: David Lean and H.E. Bates, based on a play by Arthur
Laurents
Cast: Katharine Hepburn, Rossano Brazzi, Isa Miranda, Darren
McGavin, Mari Aldon

THE RAINMAKER
Paramount 1956
Director: Joseph Anthony
Producer: Hal B. Wallis
Screenplay: N. Richard Nash, from his play
Cast: Burt Lancaster, Katharine Hepburn, Wendell Corey, Lloyd
Bridges, Earl Holliman, Cameron Prud'Homme

THE IRON PETTICOAT
Bennar Production/Metro-Goldwyn-Mayer (in Vistavision and
Technicolor) 1956
Director: Ralph Thomas
Producer: Betty E. Box
Screenplay: Ben Hecht, whose name was removed from the
credits at his request, based on an original story by Harry
Saltzman
Cast: Bob Hope, Katharine Hepburn, James Robertson Justice,
Robert Helpmann, David Kossoff, Alan Gifford, Noelle
Middleton

DESK SET
Twentieth Century Fox (in Cinemascope and colour by DeLuxe)
1957
Director: Walter Lang
Producer: Henry Ephron
Screenplay: Phoebe Ephron and Henry Ephron, based on the play
by William Marchant
Cast: Spencer Tracy, Katharine Hepburn, Gig Young, Joan
Blondell, Dina Merrill, Sue Randall, Neva Patterson

SUDDENLY, LAST SUMMER
Horizon (G.B.) Limited Production in association with Academy
Pictures and Camp Films/Columbia Pictures 1959
Director: Joseph L. Mankiewiez
Producer: Sam Spiegel
Screenplay: Gore Vidal and Tennessee Williams, based on the
play by Tennessee Williams
Cast: Elizabeth Taylor, Katharine Hepburn, Montgomery Clift,
Albert Dekker, Mercedes McCambridge, Gary Raymond

LONG DAY'S JOURNEY INTO NIGHT
Embassy 1962
Director: Sidney Lumet
Producer: Ely Landau and Jack J. Dreyfus, Jr.
Screenplay: Eugene O'Neill, based on his play
Cast: Katharine Hepburn, Ralph Richardson, Jason Robards Jr.,
Dean Stockwell, Jeanne Barr

GUESS WHO'S COMING TO DINNER
Stanley Kramer Production/Columbia (in Technicolor) 1967
Director & Producer: Stanley Kramer
Screenplay: William Rose
Cast: Spencer Tracy, Sidney Poitier, Katharine Hepburn,
Katharine Houghton, Cecil Kellaway, Roy E. Glenn, Sr., Beah
Richards, Isabell Sanford, Virginia Christine

THE LION IN WINTER
Martin Poll Production/Avco Embassy (in Panavision and
Eastman Color) 1968
Director: Anthony Harvey
Producer: Martin Poll
Executive Producer: Joseph E. Levine
Screenplay: James Goldman, based on his play
Cast: Peter O'Toole, Katharine Hepburn, Jane Merrow, John
Castole, Timothy Dalton, Anthony Hopkins

THE MADWOMAN OF CHAILLOT
Ely Landau-Bryan Forbes Production/Commonwealth United
Corporation/Warner Bros-Seven Arts (in Technicolor) 1969
Director: Bryan Forbes
Producer: Ely Landau
Screenplay: Edward Anhalt, based on the play by Jean Giraudoux
Cast: Katharine Hepburn, Charles Boyer, Claude Dauphin, Edith
Evans, John Gavin, Paul Henreid, Oscar Homolka, Margaret
Leighton, Giulietta Masina, Nannette Newman, Richard
Chamberlain, Yul Brynner, Donald Pleasence, Danny Kaye

THE TROJAN WOMEN
Cinerama/Josef Shaftel (in Eastman Color) 1972
Director: Michael Cacoyannis
Producer: Michael Cacoyannis and Anis Nohra
Screenplay: Michael Cacoyannis, from Edith's Hamilton's
English translation of the play by Euripides
Cast: Katharine Hepburn, Vanessa Redgrave, Genevieve Bujold,
Irene Papas, Brian Blessed, Patrick Magee, Alberto Sanz

ROOSTER COGBURN
Universal (in Panavision and Technicolor) 1975
Director: Stuart Millar
Producer: Hal B. Wallis
Screenplay: Martin Julien, suggested by a character in the novel
True Grit by Charles Portis
Cast: John Wayne, Katharine Hepburn, Anthony Zerbe, Strother
Martin, Richard Jordan, John McIntire, Paul Koslo

OLLY OLLY OXEN FREE
Released by Sanrio 1981
Director & Producer: Richard A. Colla
Screenplay: Eugene Poinc, based on a story by Mario L. de Ossio,
Richard Colla, and Eugene Poinc
Cast: Katharine Hepburn, Kevin McKenzie, Dennis Dimster,
Peter Kliman, Joshua (an English sheepdog)

ON GOLDEN POND
Universal/AFD release of an ITC Films/IPC Films production 1981
Director: Mark Rydell
Producer: Bruce Gilbert
Screenplay: Ernest Thompson, based on his play
Cast: Henry Fonda, Katharine Hepburn, Jane Fonda, Douglas
McKeon, Dabney Coleman

# 11

# Stage and Television Work

THE BIG POND
Script: George Middleton and A.E. Thomas
Producer: Edwin H. Knopf and William P. Farnsworth
Director: Edwin H. Knopf
Opening Night: August, 1928 in New York
Cast: Marius Rogati, Reed Brown, Jr., Marie Curtis, Doris Rankin, Katharine Hepburn (who was replaced after the show previewed in Great Neck, New York)

THESE DAYS
Script: Katharine Clugston
Producer: Arthur Hopkins
Director: Arthur Hopkins
Opening Night: November 12, 1928 at the Cort Theater, New York
Cast: Mary Hall, Mildren McCoy, Gertrude Moran, Katharine Hepburn, Gladys Hopeton, Bruce Evans

HOLIDAY
Script: Philip Barry
Producer; Arthur Hopkins
Director: Arthur Hopkins
Opening Night: November 26, 1928 at the Plymouth Theater, New York
Cast: Hope Williams (understudied by Katharine Hepburn, who never got a chance to go on), Ben Smith, Dorothy Tree, Monroe

123

Owsley, Barbara White, Donald Ogden Stewart

DEATH TAKES A HOLIDAY
Script: Alberto Casella, adapted by Walter Ferris
Producer: Lee Shubert
Director: Lawrence Marston
Opening Night: December 26, 1929 at the Ethel Barrymore Theatre, New York
Cast: Florance Golden, Thomas Bate, James Dale, Ann Orr, Olga Birbeck, Viva Cirkett, Wallace Erskine, Lorna Lawrence, Roland Bottomly, Martin Burton, Katharine Hepburn (who was fired during the Philadelphia preview)

A MONTH IN THE COUNTRY
Script: Ivan A. Turgenev, translated by M.S. Mandell
Producer: The Theatre Guild
Director: Rouben Mamoulian
Opening Night: March 17, 1930 at the Guild Theatre, New York
Cast: Minna Phillips, Alla Nazimova, Dudley Digges, Eunice Stoddard, Katharine Hepburn

ART AND MRS. BOTTLE
Script: Benn W. Levy
Producer: Kenneth MacGowan and Joseph Verner Reed
Director: Clifford Brooke
Opening Night: November 18, 1930 at the Maxine Elliott Theatre, New York
Cast: Jane Cowl, Lewis Martin, Leon Quartermain, Joyce Carey, Katharine Hepburn

THE ANIMAL KINGDOM
Script: Philip Barry
Producer: Gilbert Miller and Leslie Howard
Director: Gilbert Miller
Opening Night: January 12, 1932 in New York
Cast: Leslie Howard, Ilka Chase, William Cargan, Katharine Hepburn (who was fired after a preview in Pittsburg)

THE WARRIOR'S HUSBAND
Script: Julian Thompson
Producer: Harry Moses
Director: Burk Symon
Opening Night: March 11, 1932 at the Morosco Theatre, New York
Cast: Romney Brent, Colin Keith-Johnston, Katharine Hepburn, Alan Campbell

THE LAKE
Script: Dorothy Masingham and Murray MacDonald

Producer: Jed Harris
Director: Jed Harris
Opening Night: December 26, 1933 at the Martin Beck Theatre, New York
Cast: Katharine Hepburn, Blanche Bates, Colin Clive, Lionel Pape, Ester Mitchell

JANE EYRE
Script: Helen Jerome, based on the novel by Charlotte Brontë
Producer: The Theatre Guild
Director: Worthington Miner
Opening Night: December 26, 1936 in New Haven, (never opened on Broadway)
Cast: Katharine Hepburn, Denis Hoey, Viola Roache, Patricia Peardon

THE PHILADELPHIA STORY
Script: Philip Barry
Producer: The Theatre Guild
Director: Robert B. Sinclair
Opening Night: March 28, 1939 at the Shubert Theatre, New York
Cast: Katharine Hepburn, Van Heflin, Joseph Cotton, Shirley Booth, Vera Allen, Dan Tobin

WITHOUT LOVE
Script: Philip Barry
Producer: The Theatre Guild
Director: Robert B. Sinclair
Opening Night: November 10, 1942 at the St. James Theatre, New York
Cast: Katharine Hepburn, Elliott Nugent, Ellen Morgan, Emily Massey, Audrey Christie

AS YOU LIKE IT
Script: Wiliam Shakespeare
Producer: The Theatre Guild
Director: Michael Benthall
Opening Night: January 26, 1950 at the Cort Theatre, New York
Cast: Katharine Hepburn, William Prince, Cloris Leachman, Ernest Graves, Bill Owen, Aubrey Mather

THE MILLIONAIRESS
Script: George Bernard Shaw
Producer: Hugh Beaumont
Director: Michael Benthall
Oepning Night: October 10, 1952 at the Shubert Theatre, New York
Cast: Katharine Hepburn, Cyril Ritchard, Robert Helpmann, Campbell Cotts, Peter Dyneley

THE MERCHANT OF VENICE
Script: William Shakespeare
Producer: The American Shakespeare Festival
Director: Jack Landau
Opening Night: July 10, 1957 at the Festival Theatre in Stratford,
Conn.
Cast: Katharine Hepburn, Morris Carnovsky, Donald Harron,
Lois Nettleton, Richard Lupino

MUCH ADO ABOUT NOTHING
Script: William Shakespeare
Producer: The American Shakespeare Festival
Director: John Houseman and Jack Landau
Opening Night: August 3, 1957 at the Festival Theatre in
Stratford, Conn.
Cast: Katharine Hepburn, Alfred Drake, Morris Carnovsky,
Russell Oberlin, Sada Thompson, Lois Nettleton

TWELFTH NIGHT
Script: William Shakespeare
Producer: The American Shakespeare Festival
Director: Jack Landau
Opening Night: June 3, 1960 at the Festival Theatre in Stratford,
Conn
Cast: Katharine Hepburn, Margaret Phillips, Clifton James,
Clayton Corzatte, Donald Davis, Sada Thompson, Will Geer, O. Z.
Whitehead, Morris Carnovsky

ANTHONY AND CLEOPATRA
Script: William Shakespeare
Producer: The American Shakespeare Festival
Director: Jack Landau
Opening Night: July 22, 1960 at the Festival Theatre in Stratford,
Conn
Cast: Katharine Hepburn, Robert Ryan, John Ragin, Morris
Carnovsky, Will Geer, Rae Allen, Anne Fieldig, Sada Thompson
(David Groh in a walk-on)

COCO
Book and Lyrics: Alan Jay Lerner
Music: André Previn
Producer: Frederick Brisson
Director: Michael Benthall, with musical numbers staged by
Michael Bennett
Opening Night: December 18, 1969 at the Mark Hellinger Theatre,
New York
Cast: Katharine Hepburn, Rene Auberjonois, George Rose,
Richard Woods, David Holliday, Maggie Task

A MATTER OF GRAVITY
Script: Enid Bagnold
Producer: Robert Whitehead, Roger L. Stevens, and Konrad
Matthaei
Director: Noel Willman
Opening Night: February 3, 1976 at the Broadhurst Theatre, New
York
Cast: Katharine Hepburn, Charlotte Jones, Christopher Reeve,
Paul Harding, Wanda Bimson, Elizabeth Lawrence

THE WEST SIDE WALTZ
Script: Ernest Thompson
Producer: Robert Whitehead and Roger L. Stevens
Director: Noel Willman
Opening Night: November 19, 1981 at Ethel Barrymore Theatre,
New York
Cast: Katharine Hepburn, Dorothy Louson, David Margulies,
Regina Baff, Don Howard

## TELEVISION CREDITS

THE GLASS MENAGERIE
A made-for-television movie aired in December, 1973
Producer: David Susskind
Director: Anthony Harvey
Script: Tennessee Williams
Cast: Katharine Hepburn, Sam Waterston, Michael Moriarty,
Joanna Miles

LOVE AMONG THE RUINS
A made-for-television movie aired in March, 1975
Producer: George Cukor
Director: George Cukor
Script: James Costigan
Cast: Laurence Olivier, Katharine Hepburn

THE CORN IS GREEN
A made-for-television movie first aired in January, 1979
Producer: Neil Hartley
Director: George Cukor
Script: Adapted from the play by Emlyn Williams
Cast: Katharine Hepburn, Ian Saynor, Toyah Willcox, Anna
Massey, Patricia Hayes, Atro Morris, Bill Fraser